Coastal Shipping
INTERNATIONAL
2019

Edited by Bernard McCall

Copy number 223 of a limited edition of 500 copies

On pages 56 to 65 we include a photofeature looking at the construction of Scotline's **Scot Carrier** by the Royal Bodewes shipyard at Hoogezand on the Winschoterdiep. The ship was launched on 14 September 2018.

(Royal Bodewes)

Front cover: On pages 35 - 39, there is a description of the Scottish port of Lochaline. An important trade is the export of high quality silica sand from a mine situated on Loch Aline, with much of the sand being taken to Runcorn on the Manchester Ship Canal. From there it is delivered to a manufacturer for the production of glass. In 2018 the **Sea Ruby** (CYM, 1382gt/92) was often used to load these cargoes.

(Company archives, courtesy Veronique Walraven, Lochaline Quartz Co Ltd)

Back cover: A dramatic view of the tanker **Promitheas** (GRC, 2117gt/76), ex **Tankvik**-03, **Chess**-87, **Fredensborg**-85, as she passed through the Corinth Canal on 10 July 2011.

(Dennis Mortimer)

INTRODUCTION

From 2000 until 2009 we published what became known as "coaster annuals". These were basically photo albums with photographs taken consecutively through the year and detailed captions for each photograph. The captions gave information about the ship and the location. As the years went by, the range of locations increased and so did the quality of the photography but for reasons that we never really understood sales failed to improve correspondingly. As far as trade outlets were concerned, the absence of a spine on the books made them unpopular as they could not be displayed properly.

Equally surprisingly, since we ceased publication of the annuals, we have been repeatedly asked if we can resume publication. We are responding to these requests with this new volume which differs from the earlier ones. We have intended this to be more than a photo album so we are including feature articles in addition to photo features with much more detailed captions. Furthermore it is a hardback book which will be more acceptable to trade outlets.

A glance at the contents will reveal the wide range of subjects and geographical areas that are covered. We are very grateful indeed to all those who have contributed and we hope that readers will consider the book to be sufficiently interesting for it to become an annual publication.

Acknowledgements

As noted above, a huge number of people have contributed, far too many to be named individually. Obviously we have a huge debt of gratitude to all those who contributed articles; the book could not have been produced without them. Many others have checked information and confirmed details where necessary. All photographers have been credited wherever possible and we have sought out copyright holders (not always successfully despite our best efforts) when images have come from collections. We also extend our thanks once again to Gil Mayes for his proof reading.

Bernard McCall   Portishead   October 2018

*The story of the Type 129 container feeder ships is given on pages 49 - 53. Four of the ships were built for Finnish owners with the last of the four, **Christina**, being ordered by Oy Langh Ship, a family-owned shipping company based in the Finnish town of Piikiö. In 2007 she was sold to Gustav Eriksson, of Mariehamn, and renamed **Tingö** but she continued to carry Langh Ship containers as can be seen in this view of her on the Ghent Canal on 13 April 2010.*

(David Dixon)

CONTENTS

*On pages 44 - 48 we update information about three early classes of Russian sea/river ships. It was usual, of course, for these ships to be named with the type name followed by a number, eg **Baltiyskiy-45**, and this seemed characteristic of the highly-regimented Soviet system. At the same time, the Russians found it equally easy to interrupt the sequence by including names denoting significant anniversaries (especially communist ones), notable Russian individuals, or communist ideals. The first four ships in Project 488/A, an updated Sormomskiy design, were named **Leninskiy Komsomol** (Leninist Young Communist League), **Druzhba Narodov** (Friendship of Peoples), **Znamya Oktayabrya** (October flag) and **Sovetskaya Rodina** (Soviet Motherland). The **Druzhba Narodov** was photographed in a busy Bosphorus on 27 May 2010.*

(Krispen Atkinson)

Einar Høvding, Oslo

Scrap Dealer and Shipowner

by Dag Bakka jr

One of the many young men out of military service in 1945, Einar Høvding (1919-1997) was demobbed from the Norwegian army as a trained radio technician. He came originally from the small seaside town of Sandnessjøen close to the Arctic circle, south of Bodø.

With more organisational talent than money he was the only bidder for the wreck of the German battleship *Tirpitz*, lying bottom up not far from Tromsø in northern Norway where it had been sunk by the Royal Air Force on 12 November 1944. It is said that he paid the equivalent of GBP 6,000 for the wreck in August 1947 where she was lying in shallow waters with her port bilges above water with the remains of several hundred German sailors inside.

Høvding's idea was to start by stripping lead cables from the hull plating with the help of a small group of hired workers, divers, barges and a floating crane. From there, with the proceeds from the sale of metals, the dismantling of *Tirpitz* would become a 10-year seasonal operation until the command bridge was raised during the summer of 1957.

In addition to *Tirpitz*, Høvding had made a bloc-deal with the Norwegian Government in December 1950 for all remaining war wrecks in Norwegian waters. By now he had his own outfit with tugs, diving barges, crane and lodging vessels, and every summer the flotilla went out to raise submarines or dismantle wrecks. In 1955 a scrap yard was set up at Sandnessjøen as a base for these activities but also for ordinary shipbreaking. Høvding's main business was obviously as a scrap metal trader.

Shortsea shipping

Einar Høvding was a rather private person and kept a low profile, even though he had become known for his *Tirpitz* operation. In January 1956 he expanded into shipowning with the purchase of the 1913-built coastal steamer *Hestmanden* (935 tdw) and also ordering a 900 tdw coaster from J J Sietas in Hamburg. Renamed *Vegafjord*, the steamer was primarily used as a support vessel for the salvage business, but occasionally for general trading. The motor coaster was given the name *Sagafjord* – at that time with no other connotations – and was joined by a sister *Balsfjord* two years later. These were operated through an Oslo shipbroker in the North Sea trade.

Photographs of the early vessels are hard to locate but we have found this image of the Balsfjord at Oslo.

(Per-Erik Johnsen, courtesy Geir Ole Søreng)

Early cargo vessels:

	Grt	Dwt	Date	Builder	Outline history
ss *Vegafjord*	974	935	11.11	Laxevaag	1.56 ex *Hestmanden* 2.80 for preservation
mv *Sagafjord*	499	912	6.56	Sietas	2.62 to Indonesia as *Sang Guana*, later *Badung*, *Teratai* (1974) deleted from registers 2006/7
mv *Balsfjord*	499	900	3.58	Sietas	2.62 to Indonesia as *Balsfjord*, *Banten* (1963) wrecked 3.80, broken up 6.80
mv *Balsfjord*	1126	1874	5.63	Gijon	1.64 to Panama as *Kirksons* (1964), *Lumber Trader* (1975), *Reubens* (1978), *Cari-Cargo I* (1984), broken up 1986.

Meanwhile at Sandnessjøen, Høvding lent his support to the upgrading of the local repair yard Sandnessjøen Slip with modern equipment to build small coasters. Through the company IS Syver, Høvding ordered a 199 grt singledecker from the yard in 1961, a modern design of 116 ft in length with one large hatch and 360 dwt capacity. For propulsion a 4-cylinder Normo semi-diesel of 240 bhp was chosen.

Delivered as **Canasta** in January 1962, she was to be followed by eight sisters, gradually improved, over the next six years; all with names beginning with Ca-. By the time the last was delivered in the autumn of 1968 as **Castel**, the four earliest vessels in the series had been sold, but Høvding remained in the coastal trade with five sisters.

*We see the first vessel in the series, **Canasta**, under her later name of **Rignator**.*

(Geir Ole Søreng collection)

The Canasta series built by Sandnessjøen Slip & Mek Verksted, Sandnessjøen

	Grt	Dwt	Date	Yard	Outline history
Canasta	199	360	1.62	-4	**Rignator** (9.64), **Froland** (5.86) Lost 9.87
Casino	198	350	8.62	-5	**Bas** (1.65) , **Vaagvik** (2.84), **Dahomey Express** (2003), **Brodden Express** (2006), **Sherlene** (2010), **Divine Faith Express** (2011); existence in doubt
Carioca	199	350	11.62	-6	**Fjordholm** (7.66), **Havblomst** (4.74), **Fjordblomst** (3.78), **Havblomst** (1.85), 2004 to Tanzania
Caprice	200	350	10.63	-7	1.7.87 lost, CTL
Cabal	199	370	7.64	-8	**Nyving** (1.75), **Laukvik** (2.81), **Saltnes** (6.85), **Sentla** (6.88), **Stølvåg** (1996), **Steffen André** (1999), **Osfjord** (2005), **Hestfjord** (2007). Broken up in Denmark 5.13
Canasta	200	375	7.66	-10	**Mørefjord** (6.71), **Marmorsund** (9.84). Still in existence
Casino	198	387	7.67	-12	72 Casino, Przincess Claudia Lost 6.99
Carioca	199	375	3.68	-16	**Marmorøy** (12.72) Lost 8.11.80
Castel	199	375	10.68	-17	Lost 2.81

*The original **Canasta** of 1962, photographed as **Froland** at Horten.*

(Per-Erik Johnsen, courtesy Geir Ole Søreng)

*The second vessel in the series was **Casino**, seen here as **Bas**.*

(Per-Erik Johnsen, courtesy Geir Ole Søreng)

*With the town's shipyard in the background, **Caprice** sets out from Goole almost certainly with a cargo of coal.*

(World Ship Photo Library, C A Hill collection)

*Another view of **Caprice**, now in ballast and with black hull.*

(Geir Ole Søreng collection)

*The 1966-built **Canasta** in light condition on the Norwegian coast.*

(Geir Ole Søreng collection)

*The **Carioca** working in a British port as a cable layer.*

(Per-Erik Johnsen, courtesy Geir Ole Søreng)

*A splendid view of the **Canasta** (1966) underway.*

(World Ship Photo Library)

A series from Hungary

The two Sietas sisters were sold to Indonesia in 1962 and replaced by a 1800 dwt singledecker ordered from the Juliana shipyard in Gijón. This vessel emerged in May 1963 as **Balsfjord**, but was to have a short career before being sold seven months later.

It came as a surprise when reports emerged in December 1962 that Høvding had ordered two 1600 dwt singledeckers from a shipyard in Hungary and with several options. It emerged that it was to be a "westernised" version of a standard design built to Germanischer Lloyd class. The first sisters, **Sagastrand** and **Sagatun**, were completed in November 1963 by MHD Angyalföldi Gyareysage and taken down the Danube to the Black Sea under Norwegian registry. The vessels had, unusually, three cargo holds and also a 1000 bhp Lang Gepyar Hungarian-built main engine.

Four of the options were declared and completed in 1964, and the next four launched with Saga names in 1965, but cancelled and eventually passed to the Hungarian Shipping Co Ltd, Budapest. For a short time Høvding operated the six sisters in European and transatlantic trades. One of them, **Sagatind**, in 1967 carried out a voyage up the Amazon to Iquitos in Peru. After the first two were sold in 1966, the last four were organised in AS Saga Shipping from 1970, but sold to Cyprus in April 1971. Most of them were destined for long lives, one was lengthened and two converted to livestock carriers.

The last three Canasta-type coasters, **Carioca**, **Cabal** and **Castel** traded on until 1972/73; the final **Castel** was then bareboat-leased until sold in 1981.

At the Høvding breaking yard at Sandnessjøen more than thirty vessels were broken up before the yard closed down around 1982. Some of the vessels were laid up for years before they were taken in hand; the **Vegafjord** thus from 1964 until 1980 when she was sold for preservation. The area was sold only after Høvding's death in 1997 and since cleared for new purposes. Høvding's legal rights to wrecks had been transferred to AS Saga Shipping and after his death sold to Dag Ammerud, but with little activity.

*The first vessel in the Saga series from Budapest was **Sagastrand**, seen here at Goole. Høvding's ships were frequent visitors to Goole, often loading coal.*

(C A Hill, Dag Bakka collection)

*The **Sagastrand** was followed by **Sagatun**.*

(World Ship Photo Library)

The Saga series built by MHD Angyualföldi Gyaregysage, Budapest

	Grt	Dwt	Date	Yard	Outline history
Sagastrand	1247	1694	11.63	1946	**Petro Stranda** (09/1966), **Nerina** (1968), **Mycenae** (1973), **Georgios T** (1982), **Nada 1** (1988), **Nada** (1993), **Faysal** (2001), **Nada** (2002), deleted from registers in 2010 as existence in doubt.
Sagatun	1197	1694	11.63	1947	**Petro Hague** (09/1966), **Helena** (1968), **Olympia** (1973), **Olympia II** (1975), **Olympia II Ninos** (1980), **Demetrios Th** (1983), **Takis** (1986), **Witch** (1988), **Venture 1** (1988), broken up at Gadani Beach in 1988
Sagaland	1199	1694	8.64	1988	**George X** (06/1971), **Fofo** (1972), **Mariam** (1973), **Fleur** (1974), **Bulk Merchant** (1980), **Iseltal** (1983), **Northtal** (1986), **Sagaland** (1986), **Weserkant** (1989), **Muheddine IV** (1993), **Yassmin M** (1994), lengthened by 10 metres in 1976, broken up in Alexandria in 2005 (some sources say 2011).
Sagatind	1199	1694	8.64	1989	**Christiania X** (09/1971), **Andrea** (1972), **Lady Mostyn** (1973), **Acacea** (1974), **Bulk Carrier** (1979), lengthened by 10 metres in 1976, foundered on 12 October 1980 when on passage from Gdansk to Brest with a cargo of sulphur.
Sagafjell	1199	1670	12.64	1990	**Patricia X** (07/1971), **Pauline** (1972), **Gyram** (1973), **Primrose** (1974), **Bulk Trader** (1980), **Zillertal** (1983), **Westtal** (1986), **Westland** (1986), **Weserberg** (1989), **Alkhalil II** (1993), **Rahmo** (1994), **Baraah** (1994), **Nada** (2002), **Lama M** (2006), lengthened by 10 metres in 1976, broken up at Aliaga in 2012.
Sagahorn	1199	1670	12.64	1991	**Nicolas X** (06/1971), **Irene** (1972), **Garorm** (1973), **Ixia** (1974), **Bulk Pioneer** (1980), **Ötztal** (1983), **Easttal** (1986), **Eastland** (1986), **Weserland** (1990), **Hibat Allah** (1992), **Mehde** (2003), **Mahdi** (2004), **Al Assadi** (2005), lengthened by 10 metres in 1976, broken up at Alang in 2008.
Saga	1247	1460	65	2042	65 canc, **Tata** (1965), **Mount Pindos** (1986), **Blue Sea** (1989), **Saint Elias** (1993), **Cynthia** (1994), **Samar** (1996), **Sanamar** (1997), **Kasanava** (1998), **Geni** (2000), **Nagham** (2001), **Lijin** (2001), **Monica** (2002), deleted from registers in 2011 as existence in doubt.
Sagaholm	1247	1460	65	2044	65 canc, **Heviz** (1965), **Adria** (1987), **Captain Jalil** (1992), **Jeanine** (1992), **Lady Noha** (1993), deleted from registers in 2002 as existence in doubt.
Sagasund	1247	1460	65	2045	65 canc, **Debrecen** (1965), **Tyrrhenia** (1987), **Captain Bayazid** (1992), **Texima** (1992), **Delta Livestock** (1999), broken up at Aliaga in 2003.
Saganes	1247	1460	65	2043	65 canc, **Herend** (1965), **Mount Parnassos** (1987), **Raid** (1988), **Hasan Atasöy** (1993), **Kanlar-3** (2007), still in service in 2018.

Postscript

The venerable steamer **Vegafjord** of 1913, a veteran of two world wars and 50 years in the coastal trade, has recently been fully restored as a World War 2 memorial ship **Hestmanden**, based in Kristiansand. This summer she will again be back under steam, in the grey colours of the wartime exiled Norwegian operation Nortraship.

Images of the Budapest-built series

*The **Sagaland** was the third ship in the series.*

(Author's collection)

*The **Sagaland** under her later name of **Bulk Merchant** and with all gear removed. She is seen in the River Mersey at Eastham on 11 March 1982.*

(David Gallichan, Bernard McCall collection)

*The **Sagatind** under her later name of **Acacea** in the River Ouse on 1 June 1975. By this date her derricks had been removed but her masts remained.*

(World Ship Photo Library, C A Hill collection)

*The **Sagafjell** is also seen under a later name. Now named **Primrose**, she too had had her cargo handling gear removed.*

(World Ship Photo Library)

*The **Sagahorn** was photographed fully laden in the setting of a busy river.*

(Author's collection)

*The **Tata**, photographed arriving at Valletta, was the first of the four Budapest-built ships to be cancelled by Høvding.*

(World Ship Photo Library)

The **Adria**, launched as **Sagaholm**, was also photographed at Valletta.

(World Ship Photo Library)

The **Sagasund** entered service as **Debrecen** for the Hungarian Shipping Co Ltd. The port of Valletta is the setting once again.

(World Ship Photo Library)

The final vessel was **Herend**, launched as **Saganes**, and she remains in service as we see on the next page. It is no coincidence that all four of the cancelled ships traded regularly to Valletta.

(World Ship Photo Library)

A splendid image of **Zillertal** without gear as she was about to pass beneath the Humber Bridge on 6 September 1983. She began life as **Sagafjell**.

(David Gallichan, Bernard McCall collection)

*The **Marmorsund** was originally Høvding's **Canasta** and was photographed on 18 June 2008 at Svolvær, the capital of Norway's Lofoten islands. She was using her 4-tonne derrick and grab to discharge warm asphalt in bulk directly into local dump trucks for onward transport to a road construction site nearby.*

(Uwe Jakob)

*The **Kanlar-3**, is now unrecognisable as one of the Budapest-built ships. Now over 50 years old, the investment was considered to be worthwhile and she now trades mainly within Turkey. We see her in the Bosphorus near Istanbul on 19 May 2014. She was launched as **Saganes** and entered service as **Herend**.*

(Adrian Brown)

Coasters In Canada

Coasters, as we know them in northern Europe, have virtually disappeared from the seas and waterways of Canada. Much of the domestic waterborne trade is handled by large bulk carriers, generally known as "lakers", and international trade is the preserve of larger ocean-going vessels. Some of the small ships in the Carisbrooke and Wagenborg fleets have occasionally appeared to export grain cargoes but these have been few and far between. This photo feature shows that there was a time when conventional coasters could be seen but these have been supplanted by road haulage as has happened in many parts of the world.

The Desgagnés shipping company can trace its history back to 1866 when Captain Zéphirin Desgagnés took command of the small wooden schooner **Mary-Ann** In Les Éboulements, near Quebec City. The **Jacques Desgagnés** (CAN, 799grt/60) was built at the Zaanlandsche shipyard in Zaandam for other Canadian owners and entered service as **Loutre Consol** in 1960. Acquired by Transports Desgagnés, she was renamed **Jacques Desgagnés** in 1978. She was named in honour of the family's first descendant who came to Canada from France in 1685. Sold in 2005 she was renamed **Fairseas** and became **Granne St Anne** in 2013. Two years later she foundered off the north-west coast of Cuba.

(all photographs by Marc Piché)

The **J.A.Z. Desgagnés** was the second sistership from the Zaanlandsche shipyard. She was named after Joseph-Arthur-à Zélada Desgagnés, the great grandson of Zéphirin Desgagnés, who sailed the St. Lawrence from Montreal to Natashquan accompanied by his brothers Roland and Maurice. Like her sistership, she was built as a woodpulp carrier and she entered service as **Lievre Consol**; this was amended to **Vison Consol** in 1962. Bought by Groupe Desgagnés in 1974, she was converted to a conventional dry cargo ship. In 1997 she was sold to Madagascar interests and delivered via the Suez Canal as **Slil**. She was reportedly trading between Madagascar and the Mediterranean. Sold and renamed **A Legrand** in 2001, she was broken up in Croatia in 2003.

Before looking at ships which were acquired on the secondhand market by Canadian owners, we look at some vessels built in Canada. The first is the **North Coaster** (CAN 1387grt/46) which was built at the Pacific Dry Dock shipyard in North Vancouver. She was launched as **Ottawa Patrol** on 28 October 1945 but entered service in April 1946 as **North Coaster** for Clarke Steamship Co which was the largest operator of steel-hulled coasters in Eastern Canada in the 1920-60s period. She left Canadian ownership in 1963 when she hoisted the Bahamas flag as **Karina II**. Two years later a further sale saw her renamed **Bon Bini**. She transferred to the flag of the Netherlands Antilles with owners named as Cementos de Caribe, suggesting that she was being used in the cement trade. We have no information about her ultimate fate. She was photographed on 25 June 1959.

The **Notre Dame Des Mers**, photographed on 22 June 1977, is an example of a type of vessel which was very common on the St Lawrence River in the first half of the 20th century up until the 1960s, namely the "goélette". At first, they were wooden sailing schooners but between the world wars, many became powered and they were used to carry cargo such as wood pulp to towns along the river banks. These flat-bottomed goélettes were family-built and owned and the **Notre Dame Des Mers** was one of the last active vessels of her type. Built at L'Isle-aux-Coudres in 1956, she was 100 feet long and measured 112 tons grt. Along with four similar vessels, she was sold for trading in the Caribbean in June 1978.

The **Isabel No. 1**(CAN, 384grt/29) was built for the Donnaconna Paper Company as **Donnaconna No.3** by Davie Shipbuilding at Lauzon. Later changes of name saw her become **Martin B** (1960), **Fort Libert**é (1962), **C. De Maloize** (1971), **Fort Prevel** (1972), **Isabel No. 1** (1976) and **Carlos Felipe** (2000). She worked on the St. Lawrence River until 1992 when she was sold to owners in Columbia. She is believed to have been broken up in 2003. Incidentally, her captain/owner was Gérard Desgagnés when she was named **Fort Liberté**.

Launched by Marine Industries at Sorel on 30 May 1964, the **Fort Lauzon** (CAN, 914grt/64), photographed at Montreal on 11 August 1988, was delivered to Agences Maritimes Ltd during July. She was lengthened by 6 metres in 1965. In 1981 she was sold to Logistec Navigation, a company founded by Roger Paquin in 1952 and still owned by his family. She was sold to Caribbean operators in 1988, becoming **Sugar Loaf** in 1994 and **Romy** in 1996. She foundered on 18 February 1996 when on passage from Colombia to Haiti with scrap iron.

The **Maridan C** (CAN, 1018grt/46) is seen at Montreal in December 1974. This vessel was launched at the Hall, Russell shipyard in Aberdeen on 3 April 1946 and delivered as **Lunan** to the Dundee, Perth & London Shipping Company Ltd during October of that year. On 13 November 1958 she struck a rock in the St Lawrence when on passage to Toronto. Not only did she suffer serious bottom damage but also a fire broke out in her engine room, as a result of which her accommodation was gutted. She was towed to Lauzon, near Quebec, and laid up during the winter. In February 1959 she was bought in damaged condition by a Quebec-based company, repaired, and brought back into service as **Maridan C**. Sales in 1997/78 saw her become **J B Banville** and then **Scorpio I**. With her continued existence in doubt, she was removed from registers in 1993.

Bearing an admirably Scottish name, the **Glencoe** was photographed at Contrecoeur on 18 June 1986. Launched at Goole on 19 June 1947, she was one of only three ships built at the yard in 1947. She was built as **Teal** for the General Steam Navigation Company. On 30 November 1960, she had the misfortune to collide with the South Goodwin lightship. She was sold out of the GSN fleet in 1963 and was bought by a Canadian owner who renamed her **Glencoe**. She traded in Canadian owners until sold and renamed **Jehovah Star** in 1987. She became **Etoile de Bethlehem** in the following year and then **Iron Maiden** in 1989, her buyers presumably having a liking for heavy metal rock music. Little seems to be known about the final years of her career and she was deleted from registers in 2012.

Seen at St Johns, Newfoundland, on 26 July 1996, the **Polar Explorer** (CAN, 849grt/50) was launched at the Port Glasgow yard of James Lamont on 22 November and was delivered as **Theron** to Canadian owners in February 1950. Sold within Canada in 1980, she was renamed **Polar Explorer**, becoming **Iceport** in 1996 and **Rogue** in 1998. Then registered in Equatorial Guinea, she was presumably trading along the West African coast. Some sources note that she became a total loss in 1999 but no further details are provided. She was deleted from registers in 2002.

The **Kanguk** (CAN, 2752gt/64) was built at the Finnboda shipyard in Nacka, near Stockholm. She was launched on 10 October 1963 and in April 1964 she was delivered for trading in the fleet of Rederi Ab Svea as **Gondul**. She was sold within Sweden in October 1971 and was renamed **Silva**. In 1980 she was acquired by Canadian owners and renamed Hudson Venture. She became **Kanguk** in 1982. She grounded in Hudson Bay on 5 August 1982 and later in the month was taken to Montreal for repair. Sold to African operators in 1990, she was renamed **Aldabra**. She arrived at Alang for recycling in August 1999.

We complete this feature with two passenger/cargo ships. The **Kyle** (CAN, 1055gt/13), photographed off the Labrador coast in April 1964, has a fascinating history. She was launched on 7 April 1913 at the shipyard of Swan Hunter and Wigham Richardson at Low Walker on the River Tyne. She was built for the Reid Newfoundland Company and offered the first timetabled service along the Labrador coast. Her designated route linked North Sydney (Nova Scotia) to Port-aux-Basques (Newfoundland). In 1924 ownership was transferred to the Newfoundland government and then in 1949 to the Canadian government. She is reported to have been renamed **Arctic Eagle** in 1959 but reverted to **Kyle** two years later. About this time, however, the vessel is understood to have been acquired by the Earl Brothers Fisheries and used in the seal trade until 1967 when an iceberg accident caused her to be moored in the Harbour Grace harbour. During a storm the **Kyle** broke her moorings and drifted to the Riverhead where she remained. The Provincial Government bought the ship in 1972 but nothing was done until late 1996 when the Harbour Grace township established a partnership with federal and provincial governments, as a result of which preservation began and the ship has now been restored to her former glory as a museum.

The **Nonia** (CAN, 1174gt/56) also has an interesting history and she too started life in a British shipyard. She was launched at the Hall, Russell yard in Aberdeen on 10 April 1956 and was completed for Canadian National Railways in July of that year. She had accommodation for fifty 1st class and forty 2nd class passengers with a crew complement of 33. She was designed to operate as passenger and cargo vessel on the Newfoundland coast and was therefore strengthened for navigating in ice. Her designated route was between Lewisporte and Baie Verte. In the summer months the **Nonia** delivered mail along the Labrador coast. In August 1961 she was called upon to assist the community of Musgrave Harbour which was was threatened by forest fire. She transported 760 people from the area to safety on Fogo Island. In 1976, the ship was taken over by the Federal Department of Fisheries and converted to a fishery protection and research vessel. In this role she helped to enforce fisheries regulations within Canada's 200-mile limit. In 1983 she was sold to owners in the Caribbean. She suffered engine damage on 10 March 1984 and was declared a constructive total loss. It is assumed that she was broken up but she was not deleted from registers until 2000. We see the ship at Contrecoeur on 11 October 1981.

The Port of Porthleven: Decline and Closure 1945-64

by *Neil Hawke*

Now a tourist trap on the south coast of Cornwall, Porthleven was for many years a commercial port involved in import and export. The steady decline to final closure in 1964 is covered here, aided by photographs reproduced from Tony Treglown's book 'A Comprehensive History of Porthleven' (2017), by kind permission of Hazel Treglown. During the period of this survey there was a paltry average of six arrivals a year, the majority of which were coal imports from Blyth in particular. This contrasts the situation prior to World War II when it was not uncommon for coasters to load a return cargo of china clay from the nearby Wheal Grey pit where Cornish china clay was first exploited in 1746: the pit closed in 1932.

This article is based on various sources, as follow: the aforementioned history of Porthleven by Tony Treglown, *Hayle Harbour Records 1801-1988* (Cornwall Record Office ref. AD1175), and press reports from *The Cornishman* and other newspapers.

An unidentified coaster entering port.

Harvey & Co of Hayle bought the harbour in 1855 and made a number of improvements including schemes to facilitate better access for coasters to the inner harbour. The company withdrew from the port in 1958 but limited records of Porthleven shipping movements are archived with company records relating to its operations in the nearby port of Hayle. Some of these records are incomplete, as can be seen in the final image presented of an Everard coaster – either the *Capacity* or *Celebrity* (both 309grt/47) - alongside sometime before 1959 when the steam crane was dismantled and removed. Available records make no mention of this arrival.

Following the end of World War II in 1945 two arrivals were reported, *Empire Crocus* (341grt/36) and the Dutch *Borelli* (218grt/40) this latter vessel being better known in the nearby Cornish ports like Portreath and Hayle as *Anja*. The first of these vessels was completed at Groningen as *Dr Colijn* before being requisitioned in 1940 under the management of the Ministry of War Transport. This coaster was seen at Porthleven again four years later as

Stainton, now in the ownership of H. P. Marshall & Co of Middlesbrough. The following year saw four arrivals, all Dutch, two by the *Hollandia* (162grt/30), one by the *Admiraal de Ruyter* (381grt/38) and another by the *Zeester* (179grt/31).

Possibly as a result of post war redevelopment, the three years from 1948 to 1950 saw a modest increase in arrivals. In 1948 there were six arrivals: two Everard coasters (*Annuity* (144grt/16) and *Fred Everard* (228grt/26)) and four Dutchmen: *Saturnus* (230grt/33); *Jola* (269grt/35) (previously deployed for the D-Day operation); *Mizar* (203grt/33); and *Castor* (199grt/31). In the following year, 1949, there were five arrivals, three British-flagged and two Dutch-flagged. The first coaster of note was *Stainton* whose background was noted above when arriving at Porthleven four years previously as *Empire Crocus*. The second vessel, *Empire Punch* (325grt/42), was under the management of Loverings of Cardiff before being sold to T. G. Irving of Sunderland as *Oakdene* in 1955.

The third British-flagged vessel was *Browning* (332grt/42), previously the *Empire Reaper*, and owned at the time by the Anglo-Danubian Transport Co of London. Two years later this coaster was seen at Porthleven again, this time as *Moreton Corbet* now owned by the Kerton Shipping Co. of Hull. The two Dutchmen were the *Heron* (279grt/38)(previously deployed for the D-Day operation) and *Agiena* (333grt/36). The year 1950 saw four arrivals: two British coasters and two Dutch. The British coasters were *Goldfaun* (319grt/40), owned by E J & W Goldsmith Ltd, and the Fabric coaster *Empire Fabric (*410/44) which two years later was bought by Torridge Coasters Ltd and renamed *Torridge Lass*. The Dutch coasters arriving were *Union* (315grt/38) and *Europa* (257grt/46).

*A fine view of the Dutch coaster **Europa** and the steam crane hard at work.*

The years 1951 to 1952 were certainly quiet. In 1951 there were just two arrivals: Metcalf Motor Coasters' **Polly M** (380grt/37) (previously deployed for the carriage of cased petrol for D-Day) and the **Moreton Corbet**, previously referred to when arriving under a different name in 1949. Both vessels brought coal cargoes from Blyth. The following year saw just one arrival, the **Lady Sophia** (232grt/38) then in the ownership of D. J. and S. A. J. Bradley, better known as Thomas Watson Shipping. Once again the cargo was coal from Blyth.

There are plenty of onlookers to watch the Metcalf coaster **David M** *entering the inner harbour.*

Coronation year, 1953, saw four arrivals: the **Lady Sophia** (again); the Fabric coaster **Seabrook** (410grt/44), formerly **Empire Faraway**, owned by Seaway Coasters of Hull but sold to Everards the following year being renamed **Fortunity**; the **Lady Stella** (213grt/35) owned by the Bradleys; and the Dutch-flagged **Baltic** (249grt/40) which, exceptionally, arrived with coal from Goole.

That trade was picking up appeared to be evidenced in 1954 with no fewer than fourteen arrivals. The most frequent visitor was Thomas Watson's **Lady Sylvia** (371grt/52) with six cargoes to Porthleven, followed by Metcalf's **Jim M** (410grt/44) with three cargoes, though another cargo of coal from Goole on 19 October was discharged at nearby Penzance due to adverse weather conditions. During the year there was one visit each by the **Conlea** (261grt/39) owned by Jeppesen Heaton Ltd., **Lady Sophia**, **Lady Stella**, and two more Metcalf Motor Coasters: **Rose-Julie M** (402grt/41) (formerly **Empire Bank**

and as such deployed for the carriage of cased petrol ahead of D-Day), and **David M** (350grt/33). All the cargoes were of coal, eight from Blyth, the remainder from Goole.

The following year – 1955 – was on a par with the previous year with twelve arrivals. The total would have been thirteen had not **Lesrix** (590grt/38), owned by J R Rix Ltd of Hull, been re-routed to discharge at Hayle whether by virtue of adverse weather or otherwise is difficult to say. **Lesrix** had a beam of nearly 30' which may have made it impossible to pass through to the inner harbour. It is known, for example, that **Jim M** with a beam of 27' just managed to berth in the inner harbour. Five years later **Lesrix** was lost on passage from Goole to Hayle. The actual arrivals saw **Lady Sylvia** arrive seven times; **Lady Sophia** three times; with one visit each for **David M** and the Dutch-flagged **Venus** (291grt/35).

The Dutch coaster **Venus** *being discharged.*

At the beginning of the year there was drama when the Dutchman **Friso** (250grt/39) on passage from Par to Preston with china clay struck rocks near Lizard Point. In danger of sinking, **Friso** limped towards Porthleven where the local pilot guided the coaster to port where she was pumped out and repaired before resuming passage. **Friso** had played an active part at Dunkirk and in Operation Cycle and Operation Ariel.

Left - **David M** *once again now safely berthed in the inner harbour.*

Right - An initial view of **Friso** *entering port with an evident list not helped by the driving wind and sleet.*

*A second view of the arrival of the **Friso** but from a very different vantage point. Despite the inclement weather, there are plenty of observers.*

During the next year, 1956, Porthleven was again busy, albeit by its own modest standards. In total there were fourteen arrivals. The **Lady Sylvia** and the **Venus** each arrived three times while there were single visits from the Dutch **Solent** (297grt/53); the **Hullgate** (410grt/44) owned by the Hull Gates Shipping Co.; the **Lady Sophia**; the Dutch **Dubhe** (199grt/35); the Dutch **Gronitas** (279grt/38); the **Cornel** (353grt/38) owned by the Rose Line (Thomas Rose Ltd.); and the Dutch **Iris** (200grt/37). Another arrival was the Dutch **Tuskar**, formerly the **Friso** which arrived in distress the year before, as previously described.

Nine arrivals occurred in 1957 which, apart from 1962 and 1964, was effectively the end of the road for Porthleven. The arrivals were: **Lady Sylvia** (three), and a single visit from the **Solent**; the **Karri** (354grt/38) owned by the Newry and Kilkeel S.S. Co. Ltd.; the **Polly M**; the Dutch **Antilope** (206grt/39) (previously deployed in the carriage of stores ahead of D-Day); the **Leaspray** (199grt/32) owned by Vectis Shipping; and Everard's **Aridity** (335grt/31) (previously

deployed ahead of D-Day in the carriage of stores and cased petrol) arrived from London with cement.

Sometime after 1959 the Dutch-flagged **Frema** (197grt/31) arrived with a cargo of what may have been bagged animal feed. By this time the steam crane seen in other pictures had been removed and a mobile device used instead.

*The photographer clearly wanted to place the new crane prominently in this image of the **Frema**.*

In 1962 there were two arrivals: **Hullgate** with 420 tons of basic slag from Grimsby (the first coaster to berth for five years), and the British steel schooner **Result** (122grt/1893), which arrived to load granite chippings. Finally in 1964 the German coaster **Karl** (211grt/50) arrived with 320 tons of basic slag. Thus ended Porthleven's history of import and export though imports of coal outstripped all other cargoes: Tony Treglown's history suggests that over 100 years, 400,000 tons had been brought to the port, mainly from Blyth and Goole.

*A splendid panoramic view with either **Capacity** or **Celebrity** alongside.*

Bunkering Tankers Worldwide

The provision of fuel for motor ships has become an increasingly complex matter over the years. There have always been varying grades of fuel oil to meet the demands of different engine types. Recently a great deal of attention has been devoted to environmental issues with demands for a reduction in the sulphur content of the fuel. Over the years, bunkering tankers have become more sophisticated; indeed some are now able to undertake the blending of fuels on board.

As will be noticed in this short selection, some of the tankers have been converted from dry cargo ships, others have been adapted from oil product and chemical tankers, others again have been purpose-built. The oil companies have some of the tankers on long-term charter whilst other tankers are owned by companies which buy and distribute the products from the oil companies, thus becoming traders. The huge growth in the cruise industry has given new impetus to the use of these tankers.

Sentek Marine was incorporated in Singapore on 29 May 1993. In mid-January 2018 it was proclaimed by the Maritime and Port Authority of Singapore to have been the port's biggest supplier of bunker fuel by volume during 2017. This was indeed an honour for a company working in a port which is arguably the world's leading supplier of bunker fuel. The company also owns much larger tankers in addition to tugs and barges. The **Sentek 23** *(SGP, 1602gt/11) was completed on 6 December 2011 at the Llanyungang Shenghua shipyard in Jiangsu. In June 2017 she was the first of the Sentek's bunkering tankers to be converted for the delivery of low sulphur fuel oil. We see her at Singapore on 29 March 2015.*

(Tony Hogwood)

At first glance a photograph of a British tanker delivering fuel to Fred. Olsen's cruise ship **Balmoral** *on 25 February 2011 would seem to have been taken in a port in northern Europe but the familiar bridge in the background should tell us immediately that the port is Sydney. The* **Whitnavigator** *(IOM, 1350gt/10) was completed for Hull-based John H Whitaker (Tankers) Ltd on 16 September 2010 at the Modest Infrastructures shipyard at Bhavnagar in India. Rather than sail to the UK, however, she sailed via Colombo to Sydney where she took over from Shell Australia's* **Amorena** *(AUS, 566gt/75) as the main bunkering tanker. She left in late 2014 and returned to the UK, arriving at Falmouth in mid-April 2015.*

(Tony Hogwood)

The **Santa Rita** *(ITA, 1394gt/08) was built for Petromar at the local San Giorgio del Porto shipyard in Genoa where she was completed at the end of July 2008. Soon after this, Petromar was taken over by the Dutch shipping company Vroon and the owning company was rebranded Iver Ships. With its main interests being livestock carriers and supply ships, it quickly sought to sell its bunkering tankers and they were acquired by Ciane SpA, a well-established bunkering company based in Genoa but serving the neighbouring ports of Savona, Vado Ligure, La Spezia and Marina di Carrara. We see her supplying bunkers to the ill-fated* **Costa Concordia** *on 17 October 2010.*

(Pietro Baldizzone)

The **Santa Rita** *was the first of a two-ship order. She had not even been completed when the keel of her sistership was laid on 11 March 2008. She was completed as* **San Francesco** *(ITA, 1393gt/09) on 6 May 2009. We see her at Genoa on 18 December 2010. Dominating the background is the ENEL coal-fired power station which had three units, the first being commissioned in 1952 and the last in 1960. It was one of twenty-two fossil-fuelled power stations in Italy to be closed in the last five years although it did reopen briefly in 2017 to provide power during a planned temporary shutdown of a nuclear power station in France.*

(Pietro Baldizzone)

From the start of the new millennium, the port of St Petersburg has seen a huge increase in the number of cruise ships calling at the port and has built a new terminal to handle these vessels. There has been a corresponding increase in the number of bunkering tankers serving the port, many having an interesting history. A good example is the **Angara** (RUS, 2002gt/77). On 7 January 1977 she was delivered from the Karmsund shipyard in Haugesund as **Mare Novum** for Rotterdam-based De Haas Shipping. In mid-September 1977 ownership was transferred to Nedlloyd Bulkchem and she passed into German ownership in 1991 without change of name. Her next change of name came in 1994 when she was sold and renamed **Mare Aurum**. Four years later she came into the fleet of John H Whitaker (Tankers) Ltd and, now renamed **Whitonia**, she worked out of Falmouth on bunkering duties. She became the Russian **Angara** in 2008. We see her in the colours of her new owners at St Petersburg on 5 July 2008. Fuel is cheap in Russia and most cruise ships choose to refuel there.

(Simon Smith)

Despite the influx of more modern bunkering tankers, many of the older vessels have continued to find profitable work. The **Gogland** (RUS, 949gt/76) is one of a large number of similar tankers built at the Ivan Dimitrov shipyard at Rousse in Bulgaria. Some of the tankers of this design have been fitted with a crane on the fore section to assist in raising the hose to the required height on many modern cruise ships. Her tyre fenders have thoughtfully been fitted with white covers to avoid unsightly black marks on the white hulls of cruise ships. In the background the **Navigator of the Seas** is getting underway from the recently-constructed cruise terminal at St Petersburg on 3 July 2017. The larger cruise ships had simply outgrown the limited existing facilities at berths near the city centre. With no prospect of expanding those facilities, the port authority built the new terminal. Generally passengers are unhappy about the terminal which offers only a handful of duty-free shops and is a long way from the city centre. This makes it difficult to visit to the city independently.

(Danny Lynch)

The **Hai Soon 6** (3232gt/93) flies the flag of Kiribati, an atoll and republic in the central Pacific Ocean and she is registered in Tarawa, the capital of Kiribati. Originally named **Matsuyama Maru No. 27**, she became **Hai Soon 6** following sale in 2010. We see her in the South Atlantic off Abidjan, the capital and main port of the Ivory Coast (Côte d'Ivoire), on 9 June 2012. She had just delivered fuel to an offshore supply ship and her crew are taking on board the Yokohama fenders used during the bunkering operation. Late on 26 July 2014 she was reported to have been hijacked by ten heavily-armed pirates when delivering a cargo of marine gas oil to another vessel about 46 nautical miles south of Ghana. The ship's crew eventually contacted the owners on 3 August when 60 nautical miles north-east of Lagos. All 21 crew members were unharmed.

(Dominic McCall)

The **Awanuia** (NZL, 2747gt/09) was built at the Yardimci shipyard in Tuzla. She was completed on 19 May 2009 and arrived at her home port of Auckland on 20 August. Photographed on 1 March 2016, she is owned by Seafuels Ltd, a joint venture between the Port of Auckland and Pacific Basin Shipping, and is on long-term time charter to Shell New Zealand. In typical Shell fashion, the ship is named after a mollusc, this being awanuia porcellana, a spiral shell from the Aclididae family. The aim of contracting a new state-of-the-art vessel was to attract more cruise ships to Auckland with a consequent boost to the local economy. The tanker carries up to 3200 tonnes of heavy fuel oil and 700 tonnes of marine gas oil. She operates as both fuel storage and a bunkering vessel. Products are loaded at the Marsden Point refinery some 75 nautical miles north of Auckland.

(John Southwood)

All Change for New Zealand Cement Carriers

by *Captain M. H. Pryce*

One of the few "traditional" coasting trades still existing in New Zealand is bulk cement, now manufactured and distributed from the Golden Bay Cement works at Portland, Whangarei, North Island, or redistributed imported Japanese cement from a new Holcim Cement silo in Timaru, in South Island. In the recent two years, all the existing cement ships were replaced by either new tonnage, or by "rationalised" arrangements.

A brand-new ship was **Aotearoa Chief**, (8252gt/16) built at Janling Shipyard, China, for the China Navigation Company Ltd, Hong Kong (Swire Group), who had contracted with Golden Bay Cement to provide cement shipping services for them. **Aotearoa Chief** is painted in the normal colours of China Navigation, with black hull. She arrived at Auckland on 14 November 2016 and took over the routes previously operated by her predecessor, **Golden Bay**, loading cement at Portland, Whangarei, and discharging it at Auckland, Tauranga, Napier, Wellington or Picton. The ship that she replaced, **Golden Bay** (3165gt/79), was one of the last ships built by Robb Caledon Shipbuilders Ltd at Dundee in 1979 before the Dundee shipyard closed in 1980.

The **Aotearoa Chief** was photographed at Wellington on 2 December 2016.

(Captain Charles Smith)

Contrary to expectations, **Golden Bay** was not laid-up immediately on the arrival of the new **Aotearoa Chief** and she remained in service until 10 May 2017, when she sailed from Auckland to Whangarei, and was laid up pending disposal. **Golden Bay** was sold in July 2017 to Westerdijk Reederei GmbH & Co., Germany, and was registered in the ownership of Cement Buffer Schiffahrts GmbH, Germany. She was transferred to the Belize flag, registered at Belize City, and retained her original name.

She sailed from Whangarei on 4 July 2017, called at Papeete for bunkers on 12 July, and arrived at the Panama Canal on 2 August. **Golden Bay** passed through the Panama Canal on 10 August on her delivery voyage to Europe. However, a planned contract fell through, and she anchored off Colon, Panama, until late November 2017 before she resumed her voyage across the Atlantic. After calling at Ceuta for bunkers, she arrived at Tuzla, Turkey on 19 December 2017 for drydocking. She sailed from Tuzla on 11 January 2018 bound for Durres, Albania, and on 15 January she entered service carrying bulk cement from Durres to Valletta, Malta. The only exterior change was that the **Golden Bay** logo had been overpainted on her funnel, so that it became plain yellow.

*The **Golden Bay** swings off the entrance to Lyttelton harbour on 17 February 2013.*

(Nigel Kirby)

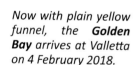

*Now with plain yellow funnel, the **Golden Bay** arrives at Valletta on 4 February 2018.*

(Michael Cassar)

Holcim Cement closed their Westport cement works at Cape Foulwind (on the west coast of South Island) in mid-2016, and **Westport** (3,019gt/75), took her last cement cargo out from Westport on 21 July 2016, discharging at Onehunga, after which she laid up there. Whilst at Onehunga, she was sold to SMT Shipmanagement & Transport, Gdynia, Poland, and renamed **Fjordvik** on 14 September 2016, registered at Nassau, Bahamas,

and after a visit to New Plymouth for a diving inspection in clear water, she sailed from New Plymouth on 22 September for a voyage via Papeete and the Panama Canal to Gydnia, Poland, where she was drydocked. Thereafter, she entered service carrying bulk cement from Aalborg, Denmark, to other Danish ports such as Aabenraa, Copenhagen, Kolding, Korsør, Odense, along with Helsingborg in Sweden and Drammen in Norway.

*The **Westport** arrives at Wellington for the final time on 16 June 2016.*

(Josh Rogers)

*The **Fjordvik**, formerly **Westport**, lies at Onehunga on 13 September 2016.*

(Jennifer Roberts)

The **Westport** was one of only two Type 74 vessels built at the J J Sietas shipyard at Neuenfelde on the outskirts of Hamburg. The other example was the original **Milburn Carrier**.

The sale of **Westport** left Holcim's cement trade in the hands of **Milburn Carrier II**, (6200gt/87), which was intended to be replaced by the second-hand pink-hulled cement carrier **Buffalo**, purchased or transferred within the Holcim group from Vietnam.

Buffalo (6311gt/98) sailed from Ho Chi Minh City, Vietnam, on 21 August 2016, and arrived at Singapore on 25 August 2016, where she was drydocked. She sailed from Singapore on

17 December 2016 for New Zealand, tested her new berth at Timaru on 8 January 2017, then sailed the following day to Nelson, where she arrived on 10 January 2017 for further work.

The "further work" transpired to be much more extensive than planned, and it was 30 December 2017 before **Buffalo** sailed from Nelson to Auckland, where she arrived on 2 January 2018 for another drydocking.

She sailed from Auckland on 24 January for Timaru, where she arrived on 27 January, but did not sail from Timaru with her first New Zealand coastal cement cargo until 29 April 2018.

The **Buffalo** at Lyttelton Won 5 May 2018.

(Nigel Kirby)

Holcim replaced the cement produced by their Westport cement plant with imported cement from Kandla, Japan, and to handle this they built new "dome" silos at Timaru and Auckland, with the latter designed to only receive cement (all cement discharged ashore into trucks), whilst the Timaru silo was able to also discharge imported cement into coastal ships for local distribution. The first overseas cement cargo from Japan was discharged into the Timaru silo on 9 December 2015 by the bulk carrier **Esperence Bay** (17019gt/10) and it was planned that bulk carriers bringing cement into New Zealand would be used to load logs back to Asia after all cement had been discharged.

Milburn Carrier II started reloading imported cement from Timaru (in between loading residual cement from Westport) and after Westport finally closed in mid-2016, she solely distributed cement from Timaru, whilst patiently waiting for **Buffalo** to replace her. When **Milburn Carrier II** was berthed alongside at Timaru on 12 February 2017, a severe southerly storm struck the port, tearing the cruise ship **Seabourn Encore** (41865gt/16) from her adjacent moorings, and she drifted out of control across Timaru harbour until she collided with the berthed **Milburn Carrier II** with her port quarter, holing and damaging a starboard ballast tank on the cement ship. It was 18 March 2017 before **Milburn Carrier II** was repaired and able to resume service, during which period Holcim were unable to distribute any of their cement from Timaru. After **Buffalo** at long-last entered into service,

Milburn Carrier II was sold on 30 April 2018 in Lyttelton to Nova Algoma Cement Carriers (NACC) and was renamed **NACC Milburn**, registered at Panama. She arrived at Wellington on 5 May 2018 for bunkers and sailed later the same day for Singapore and further, leaving just **Aotearoa Chief** and **Buffalo** to carry bulk cement around the New Zealand coast.

Where the Cement Company Names Originated

Golden Bay Cement manufactured cement from local resources in Golden Bay, South Island, at a plant and port at Tarakohe from 1911 to 1998, and their ships were operated by the Tarakohe Shipping Company. In 1983 they merged with Wilson's Portland Cement, and after Tarakohe was closed in 1998, Golden Bay no longer carried cement from her namesake region, but from a port north of Auckland at Portland, Whangarei. Golden Bay Cement is now part of the Fletcher Building Group.

The Milburn Lime and Cement Company was established in Otago in 1888. It merged with the fledgling New Zealand Cement Co Ltd in 1963, which had opened its new Westport cement works in 1958. The merged company became New Zealand Cement Holdings, which Holcim purchased shares in during 1971, and took full ownership of in 1999. In 2002 Holcim became the new brand name in New Zealand, but this did not extend to renaming **Milburn Carrier II**.

23

*The **Milburn Carrier II** at Napier on 25 April 2018.*

(Brent Hanson)

*The **NACC Milburn** outward bound from Lyttelton on 4 May 2018.*

(Nigel Kirby)

Cruising for Coasters

by *Derek Sands*

My wife and I began cruising in 2012 and initially booked a cruise from Marseille to Istanbul and back, with a transit of the Corinth Canal aboard *Arion* (5635gt/65) and originally built as *Istra* for Yugoslav operators. However around three weeks beforehand, I noticed the ship had been arrested in the port of Bar. Enquiries with the tour operator revealed "Classic Cruises" were in financial difficulties. After keeping us informed over the next two to three days it was confirmed that the cruise was cancelled and the money was swiftly refunded. We were lucky enough to get a late notice cruise with almost exactly the same dates aboard what has now become our favourite ship *Marco Polo*. This would last fourteen days with a great itinerary into the Mediterranean. Ports of call were Lisbon, Tangier, Malaga, Cartagena, Palma, Valencia, Gibraltar and La Corunna.

*Seen here in Malaga on 15 October 2012 is **Arhon**. She had been under arrest for over 10 months and was then abandoned. She was built as **Doggersbank** for Pot Scheepvaart in 1976 by the Voorwaarts yard at Hoogezand. She then became **Dollard** in 1995 and **Dogger** in 1996. She was involved in several incidents during her career. On 2 August 2005, when on passage from Egernsund to Santander with fish meal, she collided in the Western Approaches with the container ship **Sierra Express** and was taken to Falmouth for repairs. By 2008 she was **Arhon** and* *remained at Malaga until 2014 when renamed **Mamo**. She gained the name **Haddad 1** under the flag of Bolivia in February 2015. On 1 September 2015 during a voyage from Iskenderun, Turkey, to Misurata, Libya, she was intercepted by the Greek Coast Guard and Greek Special Forces at Ierapetra and arrested on suspicion of arms smuggling. She was taken to Heraklion for investigation and in two containers were found 5,000 firearms with ammunition and 49,347,800 cigarettes. She met her end in Aliaga in January 2018.*

From Malaga we sailed to Cartagena which has two harbours. The older inner harbour handles small container ships, livestock carriers and cruise ships, with a small naval base as well. The outer harbour at Escombreras handles mainly bulk carriers, tankers and larger general cargo ships with lay up facilities for other ships.

Almost opposite our berth, the Zanzibar-registered **Barhom II** lies in the inner harbour at Cartagena on 16 October 2012. The bales of fodder on the top deck should be noted. Built as **Marion Bosma** in 1977 by Suurmeijer at Foxhol, her original gross tonnage was 1,599. She exchanged her Netherlands Antilles flag for that of the Netherlands in 1978, still being owned by Bosma. Later that year she became **Atlantic Horizon** of Oost Atlantic Lijn when Bosma ran into financial problems. She changed flag but not name in 1988 coming under the Bahamas flag. In 1994 she was renamed **Baltic Horizon** under the Maltese flag.

Khaled Fahl became her owner in 2001 registering her in Belize as **Haje Azizeh** but later that year her registration was switched to Lattakia in Syria. Batumi in Georgia was her next home port when she became **Amitie** in 2005 and later **Editor** in 2008. **Omar M** was her next name in 2010 still under the Georgian flag. Obviously still a sound and well built ship she was converted to a livestock carrier in 2012 with a gross tonnage now of 2,673. At this time she was renamed **Barhom II**. She is still trading and left Midia in Romania for Beirut on 13 May 2018.

No coasters were seen in Palma, Majorca, our next port of call, and in Valencia we photographed one but she was not berthed in a good position. Whilst passing through the Straits of Gibraltar, however, we overtook several and eventually passed one that was close enough to photograph.

Dan Fighter is seen here heading west in the Straits of Gibraltar being overtaken by **Marco Polo**. In the background is the modern port of Tangier-Med which ships began using in 2007 and was being further extended when this photo was taken. It is situated 40km east of Tangier, Morocco. **Dan Fighter** was built in 1988 by Ferus Smit, Westerbroek, as **Feran**. In 1991 she became **Carolina** and swapped her Netherlands Antilles flag for the Dutch flag. In 1998 she was registered in Urk under the name **Zuiderzee**, moving to the Danish flag as **Dan Fighter** in 2004. In 2018 she changed name again to **CEG Universe** under the Latvian flag. She now works mainly in the Scottish round timber trade.

*Our last port of call on this cruise was La Coruña (A Coruña in Spanish), renowned for the swell in the Bay of Biscay off the port. La Coruña is a very pleasant place with the oldest Roman lighthouse still in use, the "Tower of Hercules", to be seen amongst other things. The port handles large and small tankers as well as smaller general cargo ships, bulkers and cement carriers. **Arina** seen here discharging a bulk cargo in La Coruña, was built as a Type 145 vessel by the famous J J Sietas shipyard at Neuenfelde in 1989. Originally the Finnish-flagged **Sofia** of 3,826gt, she changed name and flag in 2006 becoming **Arina** under the Lithuanian flag and registered at Klaipeda.*

In 2013 we embarked on board **Discovery** at Harwich for a cruise to the Shetland islands, Faroe islands, five ports in Iceland and finally the Orkney islands. Coasters were conspicuous by their absence in all ports except one. Seydisfjordur (Seyðisfjörður in Icelandic) stands at the head of the picturesque fjord of the same name. The town has a vibrant cultural scene with an arts centre, a technical museum and local heritage museum and the only two cinemas in the east of Iceland. It has a weekly ferry service, operated by **Norrona**, from Hirtshals in Denmark and Torshavn in the Faroes. It was used as a base for British and American forces during World War II and remains of this activity can be seen throughout the fjord, including a landing strip no longer in use and an oil tanker, **El Grillo**, that was bombed and sunk on 10 February 1944 and which remains a divers' wreck at the bottom of the fjord. The town located in the east of Iceland is home to approximately 650 residents who have all the necessary facilities; the rest of Iceland is reached by negotiating a mountain pass.

*At a berth just outside the town of Seydisfjordur **Brøvig Breeze** basks in the warm sunshine on one of Iceland's warmest days, 8 June 2013. Of 2,885gt, she was built by Selah Makina, Tuzla, Turkey in 2006. She was launched under the name **Ocean Breeze** and entered service as **Brøvig Breeze**. In 2014 she became **Key Breeze** and exchanged her Norwegian flag for that of Gibraltar.*

In 2014 we did two cruises, one in March and one in October. In March we boarded **Marco Polo** again at Tilbury for a short cruise to Amsterdam, Rouen and Zeebrugge. Amsterdam is of course a very busy port and coasters are frequently seen but the best chance to photograph one came as we entered the lock at IJmuiden on our way out of the North Sea Canal. Sharing our lock was the Dutch-flagged **Fiorano**, 3871gt, operating a feeder service between Amsterdam and Tilbury. She was built in 2012 by Hangzhou Dongfeng Shipyard, China, and completed by Veka Shipbuilding, Lemmer, Netherlands. She was chartered out to run a service in 2015 linking Hamilton, Bermuda, with the port of Fernandina Beach in Florida, becoming **Somers Isles** but still under the Dutch flag.

In October of the same year we once again left Tilbury on **Marco Polo** for the Baltic. Transiting the Kiel Canal in daylight was a boon for any ship enthusiast of course. **Komet III** gave us a fine view as she passed close by on 9 October as we waited in a layby. She has spent most of her career feedering containers. Classed as a general cargo ship she was now obviously fulfilling that role when photographed. She is easily recognisable as a product of the Hugo Peters shipyardard at Wewelsfleth where she was built in 1990. She has been chartered out several times but has always returned to **Komet III**, her original name.

*April 2015 was our next venture and this time we opted for Fred. Olsen's **Braemar**, conveniently sailing from our home port of Harwich and bound for Hamburg (two nights), Amsterdam and Antwerp. We were of course spoilt for choice taking many photographs in all three ports, but our most significant capture was the classic coaster featured here. Seen on the River Elbe en route for Helgoland on 7 April 2015 was **Björn M**, built as **Traute** by Jadeweft at Wilhelmshaven in 1955 and of 298gt. She became **Björn M** in 1986 and is currently owned by Karl Meyer in Wischhafen. Her main role is to carry containers of refuse from Helgoland to Wischhafen. The empty containers can be seen on deck, along with a boat on a trailer.*

In October of 2015 we boarded **Magellan** at Tilbury to set off for warmer waters. The cruise ship was heading to the Canaries and Madeira via Gibraltar with a call at Lisbon on the return leg. Having to increase speed and go far out to sea to avoid a bad storm creeping up the Portuguese coast we arrived in Gibraltar somewhat earlier than scheduled. Seen below just arriving in Gibraltar on 28 October is **Ems Majestic**.

Ems Majestic was about to berth at Gibraltar. Of 1999gt, she was built in 1996 by Harlingen Shipyard as **Daniel**. She became **Holland** in 2006 and **Ems Majestic** in 2008. On 6 December 2015 she was on passage from Rotterdam to Saint Malo with a cargo of grain when she reported an ingress of water into the engine room when in the English Channel south of Eastbourne.

Helicopters took off four of her crew of seven and emergency tugs were summoned from Portsmouth and Boulogne. The tanker **Stella Polaris** stood by until the coaster was taken in tow to Southampton by the tug **Wyeforce**. In 2017 she was sold to Turkish owners but flew the flag of Antigua and Barbuda as **Mercy**.

*Seen here in Tenerife on 30 October (my wife's birthday and our wedding anniversary) is the Dutch-flagged **Marfaam**. She was launched by the Zaliv shipyard at Kerch in the Ukraine and completed at the Damen yard in Bergum in 2011. Owned by Visser Shipping, she was officially named by Femke and Maaike Visser in Harlingen on 19 November 2011. Rather large for a coaster at 5,160gt, her trading pattern reveals almost exclusively coastal voyages.*

So on to 2016 and we were back on board our favourite **Marco Polo** for a voyage round the UK. Taking in Kirkwall, Stornoway, Tobermory, Dublin, Scilly Isles, Guernsey and Honfleur. Arriving at a very windy and sometimes wet Kirwall on 18 April, we had an interesting interlude as our patient Master tried for over an hour to get us alongside Hatson Pier despite the best efforts of the wind and horizontal rain to prevent it. Showing a vast degree of experience and skill, berthing was eventually achieved. A visit to the town of Kirkwall was punctuated by sheltering from the heavy rain showers, but interesting and worthwhile nonetheless. Coming back to Hatson Pier we had to remain on the shuttle bus for a while as the heavens opened. But a good photo was achieved of **Daroja** at the pier before dashing to our ship as another shower descended.

*Daroja alongside Hatson Pier, Kirkwall, basking in strong sunshine which would not last long. She was at that time working on the Streamline service between, Aberdeen, Kirkwall and Lerwick. Built at the Pattje shipyard in Waterhuizen in 1997 and originally named **Lengai**, she later became **Muntediep** in 2002 and **Daroja** in 2005. More recently Streamline has abandoned its lift on / lift off service in favour of roll on / roll off and consequently she has traded much further afield including a visit to Casablanca.*

Built for Jacobs and Partners in 1986 by the Yorkshire Dry Dock Co Ltd, Hull, as **Hoo Marlin** and of only 794gt, she was initially bareboat chartered to her managers R Lapthorn & Co Ltd. In 1997 she was fitted with a crane for self discharge. After the demise of the Lapthorn company, she became **Martin** in 2006. Her last owners were the now liquidated Absolute Shipping in whose colours she is seen here. She was reported sold to the Faroe Islands in 2016 and hulked at Gdynia for use in the fish farm industry.

Once again we decided to cruise with Fred. Olsen in October of 2016. **Black Watch** was embarking on a cruise from Harwich to Vigo, Casablanca, Cadiz, Lisbon and Oporto (Leixoes). Leaving again from our home port was too much of a good thing to miss. We also celebrated our ruby wedding anniversary on board, complete with our best man! Vigo, our first call, turned out to be very busy with lots of shipping interest for enthusiasts and a very attractive city and surrounds to visit. Just as we got back to the ship from a trip ashore, the **WEC Mondriaan** sailed past.

The **WEC Mondriaan** was working out of Liverpool, Rotterdam and Antwerp to ports in Portugal. I have also observed her on the Thames. She was launched for Peter Döhle at the J J Sietas shipyard in Neuenfelde as **Annabella** in 2006. During the 1990s the Sietas yard specialised in the construction of container feeder ships. Between 2001 and 2008, 51 examples of the Type 168 were built, all with a 868 TEU capacity. Of these 30 had an ice class E3 classification, 11 were fitted with two 40-tonne cranes and were designated Type 168a and 10, designated Type 168b, had no special ice classification. The **WEC Mondriaan** was one of the latter. On 23 October 2007 she was bought by Jens-Peter Schlüter, of Rendsburg, and in 2013 was renamed **Annabella S**. She transferred to the flag of Madeira in October 2015 and was renamed **WEC Mondriaan** in 2016.

And so to Casablanca, Morocco's largest city and port. It is a city of contrasts of old and modern. The people are friendly and have a forward looking attitude. The modern trams in the centre contrasting with the battered taxis and the occasional hand cart. The port is undergoing expansion to accommodate more container movements with more than 350 million euros being invested. The port's traffic is diverse and includes containers, bulk, general cargo, ro/ro and tankers with a modern tug fleet on hand. The Moroccan Navy was also much in evidence. It is a desirable destination for cruise liners. An old friend is seen here, one of two Carisbrooke vessels we were to see in the port.

*The **Kristin C** was photographed at Casablanca in fading light on 5 November 2016. She was built at Jiangyin in China in 2010 and is of 4,145gt. Carisbrooke vessels seem to make regular voyages to Casablanca.*

After saying goodbye to Morocco with a desire to return, we headed north for Cadiz. Once again this is a lovely old city with modern touches. The port however has seen busier days. Although there is an active container berth and two shipyards busy with repairs, the rest of the port seems very under used. We were therefore lucky to see two coasters at anchor off the port and even more pleased that one entered whilst we were preparing to sail, although she did not come that close.

*Although classed as a bulk carrier the trading pattern of **Grace** sees her mostly engaged in coastal voyages in the Mediterranean. Built as **Sirio** at the Ningbo Xinle yard in China in 2010, she changed name in 2012 to **Grace** as seen here. Originally Italian owned she is now owned in Israel by Haifa Marine Shipping.*

We now move on to 2017 and a "new" cruise ship for us, namely the veteran **Astoria** dating from 1948. Her history is mostly well known, the saddest event being her collision with the Italian liner **Andrea Doria** off the coast of Nantucket in 1956. She has been rebuilt twice and is now smart, homely and comfortable. Sailing from Tilbury again, we were off to the Norwegian fjords after a call for further passengers at Rotterdam. Seen here overtaking us on the New Waterway near the Hook of Holland on 19 April is **Anja** which was working on the Thamesport to Moerdijk A2B container service.

*The beautiful sunshine belies the temperature which was anything but warm and would get colder rather than warmer. **Anja** is one of the three Type 157 container feeder ships from the J J Sietas shipyard, all three being built for charter to Team Lines, one of the two major operators of container feeder ships* *serving Baltic ports from Hamburg and Bremerhaven. She was launched as **Helene** on 2 May 1995 but delivered to Jens & Waller, of Hamburg, as **Nyland** on 1 June. In May 2008 she was sold to Dutch owners and renamed **Anja** in 2009.*

*Rain and snow with fairly strong winds was the recipe for the cruise but very enjoyable still. The bonus of seeing some ships dispelled any cold with some certain beverages helping as well. Venturing out into the cold sunshine as we left Bergen on 24 April we were passed by **Artic Junior**. Although she is listed as a general cargo ship she is obviously involved in the fish farm* *industry as her EWOS hull logo shows. EWOS is a firm supplying fish feed and a member of the Cargill Group founded in Iowa in 1865. The hull of **Artic Junior** was built by Nova Melnik at Lodenice on the banks of the Elbe in the Czech Republic and of 1,918 gt. This hull was shortened and the ship completed at the VEKA shipyard in Lemmer.*

So on to our most recent cruise aboard **Magellan** departing Tilbury on 31 May 2018 with Amsterdam, St Mary's (Isles of Scilly), Guernsey, Rouen and Honfleur as the itinerary. However when boarding at Tilbury we were informed that due to the prevailing weather St Mary's and Guernsey would be missed out as tendering ashore could not be relied upon in the conditions.

Rotterdam, Cherbourg and Portsmouth were substituted. Oh well more ships then!

I can recommend cruising as a thoroughly relaxing way to enjoy seeing coasters and all manner of other shipping. As well as an insight into other countries, their people and cultures. Long may we continue to enjoy it.

Disappointingly we were unable to berth in Rouen due to a sudden strike by some of the port's dockers. So a pleasant afternoon's voyage back down the Seine to Honfleur was enjoyed in the best weather of the cruise. Seen here on 5 May is **Allegretto** at Rouen loading bagged fertilizer for Ceuta. She was built by ATG Giurgiu, Romania in 2006 to the Trader 4000 design, and completed by Bodewes at Hoogezand and of 3,183gt. She has never had another name. She had a more detailed port state control inspection whilst at Rouen with only one deficiency suggesting she is well looked after by her owners Eicke Reederei.

With Le Havre in the background the Rouen bound **Lydia** passes us inbound on the lower Seine. As can be seen she is working for the French firm Marfret and is a regular caller at Rouen's container terminal. She was launched as **Vera** at Viana do Castelo, Portugal in 1995. She was renamed **Karin** before trading commenced. **HMS Portugal** was her next name in 1995, then **Karin** again in 2004 before becoming **Lydia** in 2012.

34

Lochaline - A Fascinating Scottish Port

by *Bernard McCall*

It is doubtful if many readers will have heard of this small Scottish port; it is certain that very few will have visited it. Despite its remote location it has a long and fascinating maritime history. The small town itself is located on the northern shore of the Sound of Mull and on the western side of Loch Aline where this loch meets the Sound of Mull. This area of Scotland is known as the Morvern peninsula. Road access is not easy, the town being some 30 miles (48km) along a mainly single-track road from the mainland ferry crossing at Corran.

The maritime history of the area goes back 1200 years to the marauding, sea-raiding Vikings. The thickly-wooded hillsides and sheltered waters of the loch would have been ideal for building and repairing their longships. Their influence can still be seen in many place names. On Mull, for example, is Aros, a Scandinavian word meaning "estuary" and clearly linked with Aarhus in Denmark. Even nearer, on the eastern side of Loch Aline is Ardtornish Point, Ardtornish meaning "promontory of Thor's headland".

*On 6 June 2018, **Liva Greta** (LVA,851gt/88) makes a cautious approach to Lochaline from the east. Clearly visible on the left are the ruins of Ardtornish Castle that guard the eastern entrance to the Sound of Mull. Built in the late 13th century,* *the castle was one of the main seats of the high chiefs of Clan Donald until the late 15th century. It subsequently passed to Clan MacLean and then Clan Campbell before being abandoned in the 17th century.*

(Bernard McCall)

The Vikings were eventually defeated by Somerled and his followers, a half-Norse Hebridean warrior prince. It was his descendants who established the MacDonalds as Lords of the Isles, the strength of the clan being their supremacy on the sea which they controlled using small galleys called birlinns which were direct descendants of the Viking longships. There is evidence that over 800 birlinns were gathered in Loch Aline at one time.

The jetties and piers used by the Vikings and the Lords of the Isles would have been made of timber and there are no traces remaining. A stone structure on the western side of Loch Aline is believed to be a jetty that was in use during the seventeenth and possibly eighteenth century.

The modern history of the port begins with the construction of what is known as the "Relief Pier" very near to the entrance to the loch. Construction was started in 1843 by John Sinclair, a local landowner who had established the village of Lochaline about 1830. It was completed in 1848 by the British Fisheries Society.

Construction of the pier was financed by The Highland Relief Board which provided work for thirty-one local families who were victims of the potato famine and the infamous highland clearances. The men, women and children who built the pier did not receive money but rather food (oat and wheatmeal). The general allowance for a man was one shilling (5p) worth of meal each day although there is evidence that the weekly allowances for a man could vary between 10lb (4.6kg) of meal and 14lb (6.3kg). Women were allowed 5lb (2.3kg) per week and allowances for children varied according to age. At the time there were over 1500 families living on the Morvern peninsula but within a few years over half of them would use the Relief Pier to board small boats to take them to larger vessels and then on to a new life in America, Canada, Australia and New Zealand.

As the years went by, the Relief Pier (also called the Old Pier) became unsuitable for modern vessels, as we shall see, and by 1992 it was in danger of collapse. The "Lochaline Old Pier Association" was formed and, thanks to a combination of public and private finance, along with a lot of hard work, the pier was restored and is maintained in good condition. It continues to see extensive use by charter boats carrying groups of divers or anglers.

The Relief Pier as it presently appears with a ramp for the use of pleasure boats.

(Bernard McCall)

It was in the second half of the nineteenth century that leisure travel expanded rapidly in western Scotland. Initially it was the excursion boats which handled the passengers but the arrival of the railways in the 1880s offered both a challenge and an opportunity to expand. Oban soon became an important centre for rail and ferry traffic and a popular excursion was that from Oban through the Sound of Mull to Tobermory. This would include a call at Lochaline but this proved problematic because of limited depth of water available at the Relief Pier.

This pier had provided much needed local employment and was useful for the ferry service across the mouth of Loch Aline but the larger vessels on what had become the daily service between Oban and Tobermory had to anchor off the mouth of the loch while passengers, freight and mail were transferred to smaller boats to bring them to the Relief Pier. This situation could not continue and in 1883 a new pier was built to the south-west of the town and on the shore of the Sound of Mull. This pier was accessible at any state of the tide. Known as the West Pier, it was hugely successful and remained in use for almost a century. The former pier master's house and old post office, dating from 1899, are still standing and have been used by the Lochaline Dive Centre.

In 1930 the 36 inhabitants of the remote island of St Kilda requested evacuation from the island as life there had become unsustainable. The **Dunara Castle** (454grt/1875) brought them from the island to the West Pier so that they could begin their new lives on the Morvern peninsula. The Relief Pier, meanwhile, was used only by pleasure boats

and the occasional puffer with general cargo. By the early 1970s, there was an increasing demand for ferry traffic to the Scottish islands The Scottish Transport Group (in reality David MacBrayne Ltd) took the decision to develop what would become known as "back door" routes to some of the islands and Mull was one of those selected.

Lochaline was to be the mainland port and the tiny village of Fishnish on Mull was to be the island "port". In reality, there was to be no port at all at Fishnish but rather a simple ramp. Lochaline too would be served by a ramp as the vessels to be used were the new Island-class bow-loading vessels. The ramp at Lochaline was located in the sheltered waters of the loch upstream of the Relief Pier and this meant that the West Pier was to be no longer used. Until its closure (to be only temporary) in 1973, it had been served by the ferry **Columba** which sailed from Oban via Craignure on Mull.

The first sailing was on 1 May 1973 and, appropriately, was handled by the **Morvern**. She was designed to carry four cars, although skilful work by her crew could result in five or even six cars being carried; much depended, of course, on the length of the cars. She was soon replaced by one of the longer Island-class ferries and in 1986 the route was handed to one of the new double-ended Loch class ferries, much to the relief of drivers who would no longer have to reverse either on or off. The much-increased capacity of the new larger ferries meant that commercial vehicles could be handled without delays to car traffic.

In connecting the descriptions of the Relief Pier and West Pier, we have omitted a vital part of Lochaline's maritime history. The story begins over 90 million years ago when silica quartz and other minerals emerged from the erosion of the Scottish land mass. Some 30 million years later these minerals were prevented from further erosion by a covering of basalt from a huge volcano on the island of Mull. It was in 1895 that a huge deposit of white Cretaceous sandstone running inland from the Lochaline shore in an 18ft seam was reported. In 1923 a geological survey announced that the silica sand had a purity of 99.8%, astonishingly high, but the difficulties of exporting from Lochaline and the cheapness of imported supplies meant that the source remained untapped.

The situation changed radically in 1940 when the Second World War cut off external supplies at a time when demands were suddenly very high. Silica sand of this purity was needed urgently to manufacture the glass required for submarine periscopes and gun sights; it was also needed for the manufacture of fuses.

When the site opened, the sand was not processed on site but was taken to the Relief Pier to be shipped away by puffer. Because of the problems already noted with the Relief Pier, it was decided to use the West Pier instead and a railway was built to convey the sand from the mine to the pier where it was crushed and washed before being loaded on to ships by chute. This ceased in 1974 but has left its mark because some of the white sand spilled

from the trucks has formed a lovely beach in front of the Lochaline Hotel. From 1974, all processing was carried out at the mine and loading facilities were built there.

From 1940 until 1972, the mine was owned by Charles Tennant & Co Ltd with ownership moving to Tilcon in 1972 until 2000. Then the mine was acquired by Redland who closed it in 2008 with the loss of eleven jobs.

From June 1941 until the end of that year, almost all shipments were taken by the new **Coral Queen** (303grt/41) and **Saxon Queen** (482grt/38) although **Ulster Hero** (483grt/24) made two consecutive calls in July. In 1942, puffers started to call including **Raylight** (96grt/38) and **Stormlight** (99grt/33). Charles Tennant & Co Ltd was based in Glasgow so it is no surprise that it used the ships of J & A Gardner, another Glasgow company, to transport the sand from Lochaline. The company's first caller was **Saint Aidan** (362grt/20) on 4 July 1942. In 1941 the quantity of sand export during the year was just over 22,000 tons. By 1944 this had risen to 34,800 tons. In the early 1940s, there were only two destinations, namely Garston and Glasgow.

By the 1970s the usual discharge port was Runcorn, a short distance from St Helens, the home of Pilkington glass. Cargoes were also discharged at Garston and there were frequent deliveries to Colgate Palmolive whose premises were adjacent to the berth at Pomona Docks in Manchester. The most frequently used ships were **Saint**

Angus (991grt/53), *Saint Aidan* (973grt/62) and *Saint William* (781grt/67).

In July 1972 *Saint William* loaded silica sand for delivery to the huge chemical factory of Elektrokemiska (later to become AkzoNobel) at Bohus on the Göta Älv, north of Gothenburg. This became a regular cargo with *Saint Bedan* (1251grt/72) being the preferred ship. After she was lost, the *Craigallian* (1494grt/81) and *Loch Awe* (1537grt/72) were frequently used. When Tilcon took over, the usual callers were the smaller *Saint Fergus* (346grt/64) and *Saint Ronan* (433grt/66).

From 1997 until the mine's temporary closure in 2008, shipments were handled by Saltire Shipping, often using their own ships *Stina* (NIS, 1318grt/71) and *Neva-G* (NIS, 931grt/65). Some cargoes were taken to Larne for Eglinton

Stone, manufacturers of insulation boards. Another destination was Inverkeithing where the customer was Allied Glass in Alloa. Approximately 100,000 tonnes of sand were exported annually from the late 1990s.

In June 2011 a new company was formed to reopen the mine. Called Lochaline Quartz Sand Ltd, it is a joint venture between Minerali Industriali, an Italian company, and NSG, the Japanese parent company of Pilkington Glass. The mine officially reopened on 14 September 2012 and the first ship to call was *Arundo* (VCT, 1957gt/85) on 30 September. Since then, coasters arrive on about two or three occasions each month to load usually for Runcorn. About four times each year there are cargoes taken to a glass manufacturer in Glasgow and three times each year a coaster loads about 1200 tonnes for delivery to Lillesand in Norway.

The Lochshiel arrives at Lochaline's West Pier.

(Company archives, courtesy Veronique Walraven, Lochaline Quartz Co Ltd)

Outward in Loch Aline, the Silverthorn passes the ferry Isle of Cumbrae.

(Company archives, courtesy Veronique Walraven, Lochaline Quartz Co Ltd)

Celtic Navigator was about to start loading cargo when photographed on 5 August 2016.

(Bernard McCall)

We have so far looked at four aspects of maritime Lochaline, namely the Relief Pier, the West Pier, the ferry service and the silica sand mine. We should conclude by returning to the West Pier which has seen much increased activity in the new millennium. Before we do so, however, we should note that on 15 December 1961 the puffer **Logan** (98grt/20) sank in deep water about 100 metres north of the West Pier after her engine room suffered water ingress when she was on passage from Troon to Skye with 105 tons of coal.

For the last two decades, the Scottish government has been keen to encourage exports of round timber by water rather than use roads which are often unsuitable for much heavy traffic especially during the tourist season. As a consequence, many new jetties have been developed and others have seen a revival. Included in the latter category is the West Pier at Lochaline which has proved to be ideal for loading round timber from the forests on Morvern. Much of the timber is taken the relatively short sea distance to Corpach, a journey that would be involve travel on tortuous roads if taken by land. Regular callers over the years have included **Boisterous** (BHS, 664gt/83), **CEG Cosmos** (GIB, 1139gt/83), **Isis** (IOM, 674gt/78) and her sistership **Burhou I** (PAN, 674gt/78).

On 31 May 2018, **Liva Greta** was at the West Pier loading a cargo of round timber for Workington. The photograph was taken from the ferry, which is the only way to obtain a photograph of a ship at this pier. Clearly visible to the right is the former pier master's house and post office, latterly used by the local dive centre.

(Dominic McCall)

Kanaal door Zuid-Beveland

The Kanaal door Zuid-Beveland (Canal through South Beveland) is in the west of the Netherlands. Although still used extensively by barge traffic, it is now very unusual to see a seagoing ship on the canal. In the 1960s and 1970s, the canal was used extensively with many ships calling at a quay at Vlake on the eastern bank to load potatoes for delivery to the Mediterranean. There is now no trace of this quay. Most of the ships featured here were handling such cargoes. The exception is the **Polaris** which was photographed at Hansweert.

(All photographs were supplied by Jan Anderiesse)

The **Benimusa** (ESP, 1198grt/70), photographed on 7 November 1976, was one of several sisterships built at the Juliana Gijonesa shipyard in Gijon for Naviera de Exportación Agrícola. This Spanish shipping company was founded in 1942. Participating in the company were other well-known Spanish shipping companies such as Naviera Aznar and Compañía Marítima Frutera. It was created to establish regular services between Spain and the eastern Mediterranean, which it did until disappearing in 1985. The ship was launched on 4 August 1970 and delivered on 23 January 1971. She was sold to Egyptian owners in 1980 and renamed **Alhaleme**. She subsequently passed through the hands of other Egyptian operators, becoming **Benimar** (1990), **Marine Star** (1995), **El Barakah I** (1998) and finally **Al Barakah-1** (2001). She was deleted from registers in 2011 with her continued existence doubtful.

The **Phoenicia** (PAN, 1426grt/68) may be familiar to some readers. She was launched as **Hyde Park** for Park Steamships on 17 October 1968. That was a remarkable day for shipyards on the Winschoterdiep as three sisterships were launched, all for British owners. The other two were **Redgate** and **Saltersgate** for Turnbull Scott which had taken over management of Park Steamships in that same year. In fact the three ships were part of an order for eight sisterships. The **Hyde Park** was handed over in December 1968. In 1973 she entered Danish ownership as **Philip Lonborg** but in the following year she hoisted the Icelandic flag as **Isborg**, becoming **Sudri** in 1975. After a further two years she moved to the Panamanian flag as **Phoenicia**. In 1982 she was bought by Lebanese owners and was renamed **La Paloma** and a decade later she was converted to a livestock carrier named **Berger A**. She became **Rihab** in 2003 and **Beccaria** in 2013. She continues to trade. This photograph was taken on 8 November 1977.

Although owned and flagged in Lebanon when photographed on 6 May 1980, the **Al-Osman** (LEB, 499grt/65) had an impeccable Dutch pedigree. In January 1965 she was delivered as **Zeeburgh** from the Westerbroek shipyard of E J Smit to Wm H Müller & Co. Quite early in her career she spent time on charter to KNSM for container feeder services. It was in December 1978 that she was sold to Lebanese owners with Beirut as her port of registry and was renamed **Al-Osman**. On 11 February 1979 she ran aground north-west of Jersey. Refloated the next day and taken to St Helier for inspection, she was towed to Rotterdam on 22 February. She was renamed **Rose** in 1982 following a sale within Lebanon. In

1987 she reverted to her original name of **Zeeburgh** for trading under the Honduran flag. She was towed to Amsterdam on 15 December 1987 and was arrested there, not leaving until December 1988 when she hoisted the Greek flag as **Eleni T** and seems to have remained in the same ownership when becoming **Monte Cristo** in 1990. Her troubles were not over, however. On 15 January 1991 she arrived at Barranquilla from Isla de San Andres for repairs and she did not leave Barranquilla until 29 March 1993. She seems to have had the same owners throughout this period and became **Tropical Sea** in 1993, apparently retaining this name until removed from registers in 2006.

The **La Paix** (LBN, 499grt/61) was launched at the De Waal shipyard in Zaltbommel on 24 June 1961 and delivered as **Embla** on 3 August to Scheepvaart Maatschappij "Svea" of Amsterdam, the Dutch offshoot of Rederi AB Svea, based in Stockholm. She operated a liner service between Swedish ports and Rotterdam/Amsterdam. She continued on this service when sold to L Davids & Sons in 1969, the only change being her port of registry which switched from Amsterdam to Delfzijl. It was in early November 1977 that she was sold to owners in Beirut and renamed **La Paix**.

This photograph was taken as she left the canal and entered the Westerschelde on 16 November 1977. In early 1978 she was renamed **Al Salam I** and was subsequently converted to a livestock carrier. On 26 November 1988 she arrived at Aliaga for breaking up but in fact continued to trade, becoming **Asad Addin** in 2003. She was deleted from registers in 2010 but evidently remained in service as she had to be rescued by a South Korean destroyer on 2 September 2017. She had 32 crew and 37 passengers on board.

The **Harostan** (DNK, 499grt/70), seen on 11 December 1982, was one of five sisterships built at the G & H Bodewes shipyard in Martenshoek. In fact the total order from Danish owners, negotiated through the Dutch Conoship consortium, was for ten ships, the other five coming from three different yards. She was delivered to Danish owners as **Eva Sif** in September 1970. She became **Harostan** in 1979 following a sale within Denmark. For much of her time under the Danish flag she worked for Sharpness-based Trade Lines. As such she loaded 51 times at Sharpness, usually taking general cargo to Nigeria. Of these calls, 14 were made when she was called **Harostan**.

In her later years under this name she regularly traded to North Africa. Sold in 1988 she was renamed **Ifrane** and in late March 1989 became **Zois K** and then traded mainly between Greece and Cyprus. She arrived at Piraeus in June 1991 and remained there until early June. By then she had been sold to owners in the Caribbean and renamed **Thet**. On 12 July she passed Gibraltar and arrived at Lake Charles, Louisiana, on 21 August. From there she traded to ports in the southern USA and Caribbean ports such as Haiti and Port of Spain. She became **Tiffany** in 1992 and foundered on 26 June 1993 in the Caribbean Sea north of Venezuela.

The **Oostereems** (NLD, 499gt/66) is yet another vessel in this feature to have been built at the Westerbroek yard of E J Smit. She was launched on 10 June 1966 and delivered on 16 September to C Bos & Sons, based in Schiedam, with management in the hands of Wagenborg. On 17 June 1969 she was taken on charter by Ellerman Lines and renamed **Ionian**, reverting to her original name on 9 August 1971. The charter must have been successful as Ellerman took her on charter as **Ionian** once again in November 1972 and it was July 1977 when she became **Oostereems** once again. We see her on 19 September 1977. In mid-December 1978 she was sold to Cypriot operators and renamed **Spyros G II**, becoming **Armada Medliner** in 1979 and **Spyros G II** once again in 1981. On 2 March 1987 she suffered an explosion and fire in her engine room when on passage from Skikda to Milazzo. The fire soon spread to the accommodation and stern section. On the next day, the ship was towed to Trapani. She was eventually sold for breaking and arrived at La Spezia in mid-January 1989.

The **Caribic** (NLD, 497gt/67) was built at the Ulsteinvik shipyard in Ulstein, Norway. She was launched on 23 June 1967 and delivered in November as **Caribia** to Johan Hagenaes & Co, of Alesund. After twelve years in Norwegian ownership, she was bought by Seatrade Groningen and renamed **Caribic**. We see her on 2 August 1982. In September 1987 she was sold without change of name to Cypriot-flag operators. On 4 November 1990 she suffered rudder failure when on passage from Punta Arenas (Costa Rica) to Italy with a cargo of frozen fish. After being towed to San Juan, Puerto Rico, and fitted with new steering equipment, she was able to resume her voyage on 16 December. She transferred to the flag of Panama when sold and renamed **Askja** in April 1997. She arrived at Livorno on 31 May 2000 and was laid up there until sold for recycling at Aliaga where she arrived under tow in mid-February 2003.

The **Polaris** (DEU, 499grt/65) was an example of the Type 28 design from the J J Sietas shipyard at Neuenfelde on the outskirts of Hamburg. Seventeen examples of this design were built between 1961 and 1968. She was launched on 11 August 1965 and delivered to Willi & John Luhrs on 1 September. In mid-January she was acquired by Dutch owners and renamed **Rien Teekman** with Wagenborg as managers. Wagenborg continued to manage the ship after she was sold in May 1977, becoming **Bianca W** under the flag of Panama. Four years later she was sold to Lebanese owners and renamed **Al Salaam III**. At some stage in the 1980s she was converted to a livestock carrier. In 2007 she was sold to owners in Dubai and renamed **Falcon I**, retaining this name when sold to Syrian owners in the following year. She continues to trade in 2018. We see her at Hansweert as **Polaris** on 20 November 1975.

Standard Russian Coasters – Baltiyskiy, Ladoga and Sormovskiy

by *David Walker*

It is now a decade since the publication of "Russian Sea/ River Ships", which provided a comprehensive overview of Russian ships operated on Russian inland waterways and on coastal trades. Much has changed in the intervening ten years, with numbers of many well known types dwindling as older ships are scrapped and suffer casualties. This article is intended to provide an update on three series of ships that are well known in UK and continental waters - the Baltiyskiy, Ladoga and Sormovskiy series.

We begin with the Baltiyskiys. As with many Russian series, the Baltiyskiy series comprises a number of designs belonging to several projects delivered by multiple yards in the USSR. The series began in the early 1960s when the Gorokhovetskiy yard in Gorokhovets delivered **Baltiyskiy-1**, the first member of Project 781. Each ship was 96m in length. A further 34 vessels were completed under Project 781, with hulls delivered by Krasnoye Sormovo at Nizhniy Novogorod (then known as Gorkiy), as well as the Yantar shipyard in Kaliningrad. These were immediately followed in the late 1960s by project 781-E, a slightly modified design with an updated accommodation arrangement, delivered by the same two yards. In total, 76 vessels were completed for these first two projects for a range of Soviet owners. Of these, eight are known to be still trading. Many of the ships have been sent for

demolition, primarily at Turkish yards, though some ships also ended their days in yards in Belgium and Lithuania, and as far afield as India and China. At least seven have become total losses, and several of the ships have disappeared from registers making it difficult to trace their fate.

When Project 781 ended in 1967, so did the Baltiyskiy series until orders were placed at Finnish yards in the late 1970s for Project 613. Numerically a much smaller class, this class comprised only 11 ships. Ten of the ships were delivered by Finnish company Oy Laivateollisuus at Turku, with the eleventh coming from the Valmet Oy yard, also in Turku. Though one metre shorter than their predecessors, and built to the same beam, the new vessels had a deadweight tonnage that was several hundred tonnes larger than Projects 781 and 781-E. Like the earlier Baltiyskiys, these ships comprised three cargo holds. The first vessel, **Baltiyskiy-101**, was delivered in May 1978, with the remainder of the class following by the end of 1980. They were built for White Sea & Onega River Shipping, receiving six ships, North-Western River Shipping which took four ships, and Amur River Shipping which took a single ship. Four of the ships have been scrapped at Spanish, Chinese and Turkish yards, and the remainder are still in service.

*Delivered in 1967 this ship is an example of Project 781-E. She was completed by the Yantar shipyard as **Baltiyskiy-68** and renamed **Agna** in 2000, as which she is still trading. This view shows her arriving at Terneuzen with a cargo of timber on 7 June 2007.*

(Simon Smith)

*__Vasiliy Malov__ is the fourth member of Project 613, and for many years was the only one to not trade under a Baltiyskiy name. Originally **Baltiyskiy-104**, she was renamed **Vasiliy Malov** in 1981. She was delivered by Valmet Oy in Turku during 1978 for North-Western Shipping. From mid-2013 she was owned by VLRP Ltd, and at the end of 2017 was sold to the Kirensk River Port company.*

(David Walker)

An additional order at Oy Laivateollisuus saw five new vessels built along similar lines to Project 613. Ordered for a combination of North-Western Shipping and White Sea & Onega River Shipping, Project 620 was a class of general cargo training ships. The ships were built with the same hull as Project 613 but with an enlarged superstructure providing increased accommodation and a secondary wheelhouse, placed between the main wheelhouse, for training purposes. The ships were originally intended to have Baltiyskiy prefixes, and the first vessel traded as *Baltiyskiy-112* for her first three years before being renamed *Pavel Yablochov*. However on delivery the remainder received names of notable Russian citizens – *Ivan Polzunov*, *Vasiliy Kalashnikov*, *Ivan Kulibin* and *Aleksandr Popov*.

Three of the ships have been scrapped. *Pavel Yablochov* was renamed *Kapella* in 2008 and *Capella* in 2011, and her last movements placed her at Astrakhan. *Aleksandr Popov* has not transmitted an AIS signal since 2008.

The newest classes described herein are Projects 16920 and 16921, each comprising five ships. Characterised by a large square stern and a single funnel in the starboard side, the ships are 90m in length and have a deadweight tonnage of 3,000. In the late 2000s this was increased in some cases by raising the bulwarks to add another deck and raising the load line. Delivered in twelve months between 1994 and 1995, the first two ships received Baltiyskiy names – *Baltiyskiy-201* (now trading as *Anka*) and *Baltiyskiy-202* (as which she still trades). From the third vessel onwards, ships followed the post-communist trend of taking names for notable Russians: *Vasiliy Shukshin*, *Leonid Leonov* and *Valentin Pikul*. The five ships of Project 16921 were very near sisters, with slight differences in accommodation and tonnages. These ships – *Mikhail Dudin*, *Alexander Tvardovskiy*, *Konstantin Paustovskiy*, *Alexander Kuprin* and *Alexander Grin* – were delivered between January 1996 and December 1997. In 2014 *Konstantin Paustovskiy* was sold to Turkish owners Ana Trading & Shipping Ltd Corp and renamed *Rhone*. Her new owners had her lengthened in April 2014, giving her an overall length of 113 metres and increasing her deadweight to 4,283. All ten ships are still in service.

The Ladoga series is something of an anomaly of those described in this article, in that it is the only series for which no vessels were constructed in Russian yards. Three classes constructed between the late 1970s and mid 1980s consisted of nine vessels each, all of which were built at yards in Finland. The initial batch of ships formed Project 285, and consisted of nine vessels. All constructed in Finland, five ships were built by Oy Laivateollisuus in Turku, with an additional four vessels from Reposaaren Konepaja Oy of Pori. The ships were approximately 2,000 tonnes deadweight on 81 metres overall, and were built between January 1972 and November 1974. All of the vessels received a Ladoga name with the exception of the penultimate ship, which having been delivered as *Norppa* was eventually renamed *Ladoga-8* in 1981. Between 1998 and 2000 all of the ships were sold off, and most renamed, though two retained their Ladoga name for their entire career (*Ladoga-3* and *Ladoga-5*). At the time of writing, only one of the class remains – *Ladoga-6*, which having been delivered in June 1973 has traded for 45 years. She has changed name only once, having been renamed *Dana-1* in 2000. The remainder of the class were broken up at a mixture of European and Chinese yards between 2011 and 2014.

*Showing off the square stern and starboard-side funnel is **Vasiliy Shukshin**, the third vessel of Project 16920. Project 16921 ships have a slightly modified accommodation design, but are otherwise similar to this class. She is shown alongside Bideford at low water during May 2012.*

(Tom Walker)

*The first and last members of Project 285 are shown together in Teignmouth during 1990. On the left is **Ladoga-1** and the right-hand vessel is **Ladoga-9**. The two ships were built just two years apart, however the difference in design between ships of Project 285 by the two yards involved in construction is clear. **Ladoga-1** has a much more prominent superstructure, while **Ladoga-9** has a more substantial forecastle.*

(Tom Walker)

In May 1978 the first in a new class of ten ships, **Ladoga-10**, was delivered. The new class was constructed as the successor to Project 285. Like its predecessor, Project 289 comprised ships built by Rauma-Repola Oy at their yards in Uusikaupunki, which delivered eight hulls, and Savonlinna, which delivered the remaining two vessels. The class was completed with the delivery of **Ladoga-19** in January 1980. The design was heavily influenced by that of Project 285, utilising the same hull design. The principal difference was that the wheelhouse was raised by the addition of an extra deck. All ten vessels were built for North-Western River Shipping, and four of the ships are still in service. Five have been scrapped by a mixture of Turkish, Bulgarian, Latvian and Lithuanian breakers; after forty years, one of them – **Ladoga-11** – is still trading under her original name. Those ships that are still trading are to be found in European and Mediterranean waters. In early 2018, one of them (**Ladoga-17**, by then trading as **Andromeda**) hit the headlines when she was arrested by Greek authorities for carrying explosives destined for Libya.

*Seen heading west along the Kiel Canal on 1 July 2007 is **Ladoga-11**, the only member of Project 289 still trading under her original name. She was delivered in July 1987 for North-Western River Shipping Co, for whom she was still trading at the time of this photograph. At the end of 2007 she was sold to her current owners, Belomorskaya Carrying Expedition Co Ltd. She remains under the Russian flag.*

(Koos Goudriaan)

If the five vessels of Project 620 are not the most distinctive covered in this article then those of the final Ladoga class, Project 787, certainly are. Again constructed by Rauma-Repola Oy, Project 787 comprised seven vessels from their Uusikaupunki yard and an additional unit from Savonlinna. They were named **Ladoga-101** to **Ladoga-108**. Built to a different hull design featuring a square stern, their most distinguishing feature was a forward-mounted hydraulic wheelhouse. The ships, delivered within a year between May 1988 and May 1989 for North-Western Shipping, were built with a deadweight tonnage of 2,075 on a length of 82.5 metres and with a capacity of 84 containers.

All of these ships lost their Ladoga prefix in 2007 and 2008, however with the exception of two, all are still in service. **Ladoga-102** and **Ladoga-103** remained together throughout their careers, being renaming **Yeya-1** and **Yeya-2** for Yeya Shipping Ltd in August and June 2008, respectively, and then again to **Cabrana** and **Sagitta** for Norvik Branka JSC the following June. They were eventually sold for scrap by Gemi Yan Sanayi ve Ticaret AS, and both arrived at Aliaga on 28 May 2012.

Both in terms of size of vessel and the number of ships, the largest series covered in this article is the Sormovskiy series. Comprising five projects and a total of 156 ships, the first Sormovskiy vessels were constructed in the late 1960s. The first Sormovskiy class was Project 1557, and comprised 122 ships built between the Krasnoye Sormovo yard at Nizhny Novogorod and the Volodarskogo yard at Rybinsk from the late 1960s until the early 1980s. The final vessel in the class was delivered in July 1986 as **Sormovskiy-53** at Nizhny Novogorod.

The ships were 114 metres in length and had four holds. At the time of writing approximately half of the ships are still in service. Some have been broken up, and eleven have been declared a total loss.

Alongside the final units of Project 1557 the Ivan Dimitrov yard at Rousse delivered nine ships, which formed Project 614. With a length overall of 114 metres and a deadweight of just over 3,000 tonnes, the ships were delivered between 1981 and early 1983 for a mixture of Russian and Bulgarian owners. The Russian ships were delivered as **Sormovskiy-3001** to **Sormovskiy-3007**, omitting **Sormovskiy-3005**, while the Bulgarian ships were named **Kavarna**, **Sozopol** and **Pomorie** (all three were renamed in 2008 and 2009). All nine of the vessels remain in service – at the time of writing, all were operating in the eastern Mediterranean and Black Sea areas.

The distinctive outline of Project 787 is evident in this image of **Ladoga-108** at anchor off Istanbul on 20 September 2004. The design was ideal for the carriage of project cargoes on deck as seen here.

(Martin Penwright)

In the late 1970s four vessels were ordered from the shipyard at Viana do Castelo in Portugal. Denoted Project 488/A, these vessels and the subclasses that followed are the only ships in this article constructed in western Europe.

The first four vessels, Project 488/A, were delivered in the late 1970s for United Volga Shipping Co, and were built to slightly larger dimensions than their predecessors at 119 metres in length. None of the vessels carried Sormovskiy names, being named **Leninskiy Komsomol**, **Druzhba Narodov**, **Znamya Oktyabrya** and **Sovetskaya Rodina**.

Between 1982 and 1985 United Volga Shipping Co ordered two more subclasses from Viana do Castelo – Projects 488/AM and 488/AM2. The three vessels of Project 488/AM, delivered in late 1982 and early 1983, were all named after anniversaries deemed significant in Russia: **XVII Syezd Profsoyuzov** (17th Trade Union Congress), **XI Pyatiletka** (11th Five-Year Plan) and **65 Let Sovetskoy Vlasti** (65 Years of Soviet Power). On the collapse of the USSR, the three ships were given Sormovskiy names, **Sormovskiy-3048**, **Sormovskiy-3049** and **Sormovskiy-3050**.

Two members of the Sormovskiy series, **Sormovskiy 3050** and **Sormovskiy 3051**, under construction at the Viana do Castelo yard in Portugal. The photograph was supplied by the yard to the late Chris Cheetham to whom we are indebted for his research work on sea/river ships.

(David Walker collection)

Project 488/AM2 comprised four vessels and returned to the Sormovskiy prefix with vessels named **Sormovskiy-3051** to **Sormovskiy-3054**. At the time of writing all four vessels retain their original names. 1986 and 1987 saw the delivery of Project 488/AM3, five vessels in total (four for North-Western River Shipping and one for White Sea & Onega River Shipping). The ships were delivered as the range **Sormovskiy-3055** to **Sormovskiy-3059**, and with the exception of **Sormovskiy-3059** (which was renamed **Aleksandr Shotman** in 1999 and then **Mechta S** in 2013) all are trading under those names today. Differences between Projects 488/AM, 488/AM2 and 488/AM3 are slight, and a more noticeable change came about with the introduction of Project 488/AM4. These nine vessels featured a modified accommodation, with a single mast post replacing the twin mast arrangement used on the earlier classes, as well as the addition of a drop-down lifeboat.

All but three of the ships were delivered with Sormovskiy names, **Sormovskiy-3060** to **Sormovskiy-3068**. The three that did not were delivered as **Buniyat Sardarov**, **Gezenfer Musabeyov** and **Pyotr Anokhin**. The ships were ordered for all six of the major Russian river-sea operators, as well as for Azerbaijan State Caspian Shipping Co. With the delivery of **Sormovskiy-3068** for Northern River Shipping Co in November 1991, the Sormovskiy series came to a close. All of Project 488/A and its subclasses remain in service.

This article has covered three of the well known series of Russian river sea ships operated since the 1970s. Given the longevity some of the earlier vessels have shown, it seems likely that the newer ships described will be in service for many years to come.

*Shown at Teignmouth on 9 March 2010 is **Sormovskiy-3003**, an example of Project 614. Built at Rousse in 1981, she was in her thirtieth year of trading under her original name when photographed, and the following year was renamed **Savite**. This name lasted only two years, and at the end of 2013 she was again renamed **Sormovo-2**, as which she is still in service.*

(David Walker)

*The **Vasiliy Kalashnikov** was in poor external condition when photographed at St Petersburg on 2 July 2011. She is one of the five examples of the Project 620 design and the extra wheelhouse used in the training of cadets is clearly visible.*

(Koos Goudriaan)

Sietas Type 129 Container Feeders

by *Simon Smith*

The prolific J J Sietas shipyard at Hamburg-Neunfelde is well known for producing coasters and feeder containerships. A typical class is the Type 129, sixteen of which were delivered between 1985 and 1991. Built primarily for German owners operating in the short sea container trades like many Sietas-built vessels they have come to be spread far and wide for owners in the Mediterranean and Far East.

The first vessel, yard number 931, was the **Wega** which was launched in November 1985 and delivered to Hans-Peter Wegener a month later. Deliveries soon followed to other German owners including Johann Kahrs, Helmut Funck, Gebrüder Winter and Gerd Bartels. Some of the ships were launched as named by their owners but entered service under the name chosen by the charterer. Four of the type designated 129a were delivered to Finnish operator Rederi Engship AB in 1991. They had an Ice Class 1A classification.

Although constructed for container trades the ships were built without cell guides and had two box-shaped holds with hydraulically-operated folding hatch covers. Length overall was 103,5 metres with a 16 metre beam. Container capacity for the first three in the series, built in 1985/86, was 341 TEU which was increased to 372 TEU for the remaining thirteen ships all built in 1990/91. Machinery installed in these vessels consisted of a four stroke MAK or Wärtsilä diesel engine.

Feeder operators included ARA, Containerships, DFDS, Gracechurch Lines, Maersk, Manchester Liners, Team Lines and Unifeeder. As feeder ships grew in size during the 1990s and the German operators re-equipped with newer ships, the Type 129s were acquired by owners in the Mediterranean and Far East. Four of the class were acquired by Indonesian operators. Two of these are known to have been demolished in Indonesia and a third (**Sweet Istanbul**) sank off Tanjung Priok in 2017. It is likely that the last of the quartet, **Bintang Jasa 33**, has also been recycled locally.

Twelve vessels remain in trade of which two (**Avrora** and **Uliss**) operate under the Russian flag for Poseidon Shipping. The other ten are registered in Sierra Leone (4), Togo (4), Comoros Islands (1) and Panama (1) and trade in the Black Sea and Mediterranean. The last of the series, yard number 1061, has been converted to a livestock carrier operating as **Omega Star** for a Liberian-registered company.

The first of the ships delivered to Engship as **Smaragden** gained notoriety in 2014. Sailing from Ravenna in poor visibility as **Lady Aziza**, she collided with the Turkish general cargo ship **Gokbel** resulting in the sinking of the Turkish ship with the loss of six of her eleven crew. Having been auctioned at Ravenna in early 2018 she was renamed **Yahya Junior** and sailed under tow of **Christos XXIV** in July bound for Alexandria. Her purchasers are reported to be Medway Marine.

*The first ship of the design was delivered to Hans-Peter Wegener as **Wega**. We see her later in her career when named **Marina**. She was passing Hochdonn on the Kiel Canal on 29 June 2007.*

(Koos Goudriaan)

Vessel	Yard No.	IMO No.	Launch	Original owner	Later names & year of change	Status
Wega	931	8509818	4/11/85	Hans-Peter Wegener	96-**Tina**, 01-**Marina de Alcudia**, 03-**Marina**, 05-**Karsnes**, 06-**Marina**, 09-**Jaohar Challenger**, 17-**Captain Yusif**	S
Uwe Kahrs	976	8504258	19/10/85	Johann Kahrs	86-**Gracechurch Gem**, 88-**Uwe Kahrs**, 90-**Maersk Tinto**, 91-**Meteor**, 95-**Fenja**, 03-**Sea Vita**, 08-**Avrora**	S
Käte (lchd)	977	8603547	17/11/86	Helmut Funck	86-**Containerships II**, 90-**Kaete**, 96-**Kate**, 96-**Tanja**, 14-**Sea Explorer**	S
Cimbria (lchd)	1034	8913045	30/1/91	Gebrüder Winter	91-**Dana Sirena**, 91-**Lloyd Iberia**, 92-**Cimbria**, 93-**Churruca**, 96-**Rhein Carrier**, 11-**Uliss**	S
Corvette (lchd)	1035	8913057	20/2/91	Gebrüder Winter	91-**Dana Corvette**, 91-**Lloyd Scandinavia**, 92-**Corvette**, 94-**CMBT Corvette**, 99-**Portlink Corvette**, 05-**Eldorado**, 06-**Somers Isles**, 13-**Noura M**, 17-**King Victor**	S
Sven Dede (lchd)	1043	8913069	26/3/91	Friedhelm Dede	91-**Gracechurch Harp**, 01-**Sven Dede**, 01-**Gracechurch Moon**, 02-**Sven Dede**, 04-**Admiral Rainbow**, 07-**Marti Prime**	BU
Nincop	1044	8913021	12/12/90	Gerd Bartels	91-**City of Valletta**, 92-**Nincop**, 93-**Norasia Alexandria**, 95-**Nincop**, 95-**OPDR Tejo**, 99-**Nincop**, 02-**Portlink Sprinter**, 04-**Hajo**, 15-**Amira Leen**	S
Francop	1045	8913033	15/2/91	Gerd Bartels	91-**Manchester Trader**, 92-**Francop**, 94-**Rhein Lagan**, 94-**Emma**, 96-**CMBT Cutter**, 96-**Aquitaine Spirit**, 97-**Francop**, 03-**Tossens**, 07-**ARA Felixstowe**, 12-**Bintang Jasa 33**	Q
Merkur	1053	9015981	20/4/91	Gerd Bartels	05-**ARA Zeebrugge**, 14-**Jaohar Adam**	S
Rhein Trader	1056	8913071	9/3/91	Engelbert Schepers	93-**Rhein Lee**, 93-**Rhein Trader**, 02-**Portlink Tracer**, 03-**Annette**, 11-**Rhein**, 13-**Basel S4**, 17-**Jaohar Ravenna**	S
Zenit	1057	9015993	13/5/91	Bernd Bartels	91-**Gracechurch Crown**, 02-**Zenit**, 04-**Elegance**, 04-**Bermuda Islander**, 07-**Elegance**, 10-**Sweet Istanbul**	TL
Smaragden	1058	8917716	20/8/91	Engship	07-**Soave**, 14-**Lady Aziza**, 18-**Yahya Junior**	S
Passaden	1059	8917728	11/9/91	Engship	92-**ECL Captain**, 92-**Passaden**, 07-**Sereno**, 14-**Jaohar Livia**	S
Klenoden	1060	8917730	1/10/91	Engship	14-**Leo I**	S
Christina	1061	8917742	23/10/91	Engship	07-**Tingo**, 15-**Basel S6**, 17-**Omega Star**	S
Schleswig-Holstein	1066	9014365	30/5/91	Claus Speck	91-**ECL Commander**, 91-**Nordic Bridge**, 94-**Gracechurch Planet**, 96-**Holstein**, 05-**Macau**	BU

Abbreviations

lchd - name when launched
S - in service
BU - broken up
Q - status unknownw
TL - total lossW

The only ship in the series to have been delivered to Helmut Funck was launched as **Käte** but entered service as **Containerships II** for her charterer. We see her on the New Waterway on 23 June 2012 when she was in Dutch ownership as **Tanja**.

(Simon Smith)

The **Rhein Carrier** was the first of two ships ordered by Gebrüder Winter. Launched as **Cimbria**, she too entered service under the name of her charterer. In her case she had been chartered by DFDS and was named **Dana Sirena**. Again on the New Waterway, she was passing Rozenburg on 14 June 2008.

(Simon Smith)

The **Rhein** was delivered as **Rhein Trader** to Reederei Kiepe-Schepers, a company established in 1974 and controlled at the time by Engelbert Schepers, a member of a well-known shipping family from Haren/ Ems. The ship initially worked for Rheintainer Line. With her hull showing evidence of ice navigation on the waterline and then named **Rhein** the ship was approaching Albert Dock, Hull, from St Petersburg on 18 February 2012.

(Simon Smith)

The **ARA Zeebrugge** enters the port of Zeebrugge on 1 June 2006 at the end of a voyage from Le Havre. She departed for Immingham on the following day. She was the last of the three ships delivered to Gerd Bartels.

(Simon Smith)

The **ARA Zeebrugge** is relatively unusual in having only three names during her career. Built as **Merkur**, she became **ARA Zeebrugge** in 2005 and then **Jaohar Adam** in 2014. We see her thus named at Alexandria on 22 April 2015 as she was discharging her cargo of timber to a barge. It should be noted that she still had an ARA funnel design.

(Tony Hogwood)

All four ships delivered to Engship were given white hulls. The **Smaragden** was the first of the four and was photographed as she approached Felixstowe on 8 January 2006. Although she and her three sisters were built to trade between Germany and Finland, she was completing a service that had seen her linking Rotterdam to Dunkirk, Le Havre and Felixstowe. She moved to a new route linking Hamburg and Bremerhaven to Kaliningrad.

(Simon Smith)

In 2007 the **Smaragden** was sold to Dutch owners and renamed **Soave**. She was taken on long-term charter by Swedish operator Percy Österström, based in Norrköping, and used on the Pal Line service connecting Goole (and later Hull) to ports in eastern Sweden. She was photographed as she left Albert Dock, Hull, and entered the River Humber with assistance from John Dean's tug **Lashette** on 14 May 2014.

(Simon Smith)

The **Passaden** was the second of the Engship vessels and in 2007 she was sold to the same Dutch company as sister vessel **Smaragden**. Renamed **Sereno**, she too was taken on long-term charter by Percy Österström and used on the Pal Line service. She is seen in the River Humber as she moved from Albert Dock to King George Dock at Hull on 29 June 2013. By this time Pal Line had merged with TransAtlantic and was marketed as TransPal Line.

(Simon Smith)

It is the third of the Engship vessels, **Klenoden**, which has had fewest changes of identity. The solitary change came in 2014 when she was bought by owners based in Alexandria and renamed **Leo I**. She trades between Mediterranean and Black Sea ports, often in the Ukraine, and so is regularly seen in the Bosphorus. When photographed northbound in that busy waterway on 3 August 2015, however, she was on passage from Izmit to Batumi.

(Simon Smith)

The Birth of a Modern Coaster

by *Bernard McCall*

The vast majority of readers will not have had any opportunity to visit a modern shipyard so we are delighted that Scotline and the Royal Bodewes shipyard have allowed us to look at some aspects of the construction of the new ***Scot Carrier*** which was launched at the shipyard on 14 September 2018. Except where credited otherwise, all photographs were taken by Mark Thompson of Intrada

Ships Management which looks after the technical, commercial and administrative management of the vessels operated by Scotline. The ships are owned by Scotline Mariner Holdings which is simplified to Scotline for branding purposes. We are very grateful indeed to Mark, to Scotline, and to the Royal Bodewes shipyard for making these photographs available to us.

It must be borne in mind that modern ships are built in sections, some of which are fabricated in various parts of the site. A Mammoet low loader is used to move the sections to the location where they are required.

The bow section is starting to take shape and a welder is working in the area of the bow thruster.

The wheelhouse is constructed separately and will be lifted on to the ship by crane later.

The engine room is also starting to take shape. Obviously much of the pipework must be fitted as construction makes progress.

The aftermost part of the ship is also fabricated separately and will later be craned on. This image shows the detailed calculation for the lettering. Careful observation of the background will prove that this section is constructed upside down.

In the meantime work is going on in the accommodation areas with Rockwool acoustic insulation panels being fitted.

There are, of course, many individual items of equipment that must be purchased, delivered and be ready for fitting at the appropriate time during construction.

Left: the emergency generator.

Below left: the MAK engine is ready to be lifted into position on the ship.

Below right: the packing slip for the engine which also provides basic information.

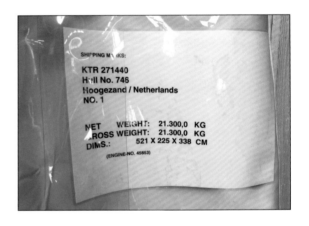

The gearbox awaits connection.

An unusual opportunity to observe a bow thruster unit from within the tunnel.

A Lloyd's Register surveyor checks the ship's draught marks.

The stern section of the ship is moved carefully out of the construction hall and on to the quayside using the 16 axle lines of an SPMT (self-propelled modular transporter) supplied by Wagenborg Nedlift.

*With only limited space available for turning, the stern section is now in position on the quayside. The vessel already launched and being fitted out is **Arklow Villa**.*

The SPMT is now being used to move the midships section out of the construction hall. This photo clearly illustrates the very limited space available on the quayside to turn the load.

Preparations are made to line up the midships section with the aft section.

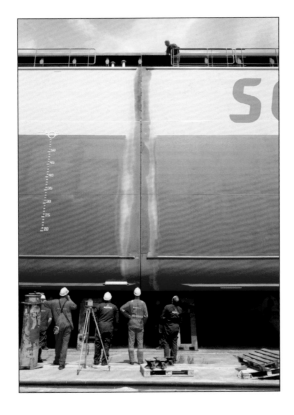

Staff from the Royal Bodewes yard and from Wagenborg Nedlift are monitoring the alignment very carefully. When this photograph was taken the two sections were only millimetres apart. The almost imperceptible difference in height would be eliminated before the two sections were joined permanently.

Now perfectly aligned, the two sections have been joined together. At this stage, all that remains is for the bow section to be attached and the superstructure to be completed.

The bow section is being positioned in readiness for joining to the rest of the ship. Hydraulic jacks will be used to raise the bow section to the correct height.

The propeller and tail shaft are now ready for fitting.

Meanwhile on the ship preparations are made to fit the tail shaft and propeller into the stern tube.

The propeller and tail shaft are being fitted into the stern tube.

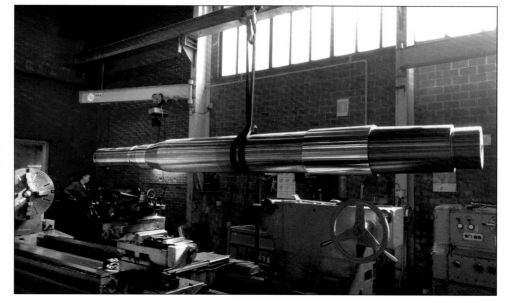

The rudder stock was manufactured by Benes, a specialist manufacturer of such equipment based locally in Hoogezand.

The rudder stock is now made ready for fitting.

One would imagine that the fitting of wiring in such a confined space as a ship's wheelhouse would be a challenge for many electricians.

At last the day of the launch, 14 September, has arrived and the attention of the invited guests is temporarily drawn away from the ship as they listened to short speeches.

(Royal Bodewes)

At the appointed time, 12.45pm, the ship was launched by her godmother, Mrs Pat Dickie. The champagne bottle has been released and is on its way .... *(Royal Bodewes)*

... to duly smash against the ship's hull with unerring accuracy. *(Royal Bodewes)*

The shipyard was open to the public on the day of the launch.

(Royal Bodewes)

The launch. A perfect image of the ship as she meets her element for the first time with tugs taking up position to steady the ship in the narrow fairway.

(Royal Bodewes)

Within seconds the two tugs have the powerless ship under control and they begin to ease her to the quayside for outfitting work to commence.

(Royal Bodewes)

The Port of Leith

by *Alan Dowie*

Port History

Leith is the seaport for Edinburgh, on the southern shores of the Firth of Forth. Whilst its history can be traced back to the twelfth century, tidal restrictions meant that it was not until the mid-1800s that new port facilities encouraged local shipping companies to introduce steamers on coastal and near-sea routes. Amongst these local companies was George Gibson & Company (established 1797) which brought into service their first crew steamer for sailings to Rotterdam. Gibson's liner trade was to last until 1968, by which time they were focusing on liquified gas carriers. Other long-lasting shipping lines established in the late 1800s were Christian Salvesen, trading to Norway and the Baltic, and AF Henry & MacGregor, which traded coal and stone from the Firth of Forth and the Tay to southern English ports, bringing back cargoes of bagged cement.

The first half of the twentieth century saw continuing development of the port, including the creation of the Western Harbour area to add to the existing Victoria, Edinburgh, Albert and Imperial docks. Included in the Western Harbour were two deep-water berths completed in 1952 to serve the new flour mill. By this time coal exports had fallen from 600,000 tons at the outbreak of the Second World War to 400,000 tons and were to decrease further to 26,000 tons by 1962.

Like many other ports, patterns of trade were changing at Leith. A new set of lock gates was introduced in 1969, thus enclosing the whole of the port area. By the 1970s new industries were emerging, such as steel pipe coating for the gas and oil industry. A quay in the Albert Dock was altered to accommodate a general cargo service to the oil terminal Sullom Voe, Shetland. In the adjacent berth, a purpose-built container gantry crane was installed for the regular shuttle service to Rotterdam. In the Imperial Dock, the myriad of coal hoists had long since been replaced by modern shore cranes.

Other aspects of the port were changing too. The Robb Caledon shipyard was finally closed in 1983, to be replaced by the modern Ocean Terminal shopping centre, which is also home to the royal yacht Britannia. The shipyard company was founded on 1 April 1918 by Henry Robb, a former yard manager for Ramage & Ferguson. Robbs grew by buying berths from Hawthorns in 1924, the business of Cran and Somerville in 1926 and the yards of Ramage and Ferguson in 1934. The site became known as Victoria Shipyard.

In 1968 Robbs merged with the Caledon Shipbuilding & Engineering Company of Dundee, forming Robb Caledon Shipbuilding, and in 1969 the new company took over the Burntisland Shipbuilding Company in Fife. In 1977, under the provisions of the Aircraft and Shipbuilding Industries Act 1977, Robb Caledon was nationalised as part of British Shipbuilders. The Caledon yard in Dundee closed in 1981. Robbs yard in Leith survived two more years, closing in 1983.

Amongst the significant number of coasters built by Robbs were five diesel cargo ships for the Ellerman Wilson Line: yard Nos. 495 *Salerno* (1559gt/65), 496 *Salmo* (1523gt/67), 497 *Sorrento* (1525gt/67), 498 *Silvio* (1523gt/67), and 499 *Sangro* (1523gt/68). The yard also supplied coastal tankers *Hamble* and *Killingholme* (both 1182gt/64) for Shell-Mex & BP, Yard Nos 486 and 487, along with the LPG tanker *Borthwick* (1569gt/77) for local shipowner George Gibson & Company in 1977, yard no. 512.

Snapshot of coastal shipping at Leith in the early 1970s

An overview of coastal shipping at Leith during the early 1970s serves to illustrate how trades have changed over the years.

The writer recalls a very busy port during the early 1970s, with all docks being well utilised. In the Edinburgh Dock, a liner service was operated to Thorshavn in the Faroe Islands, regular callers included the *Heykur* (FRO, 299grt/72), *Rokur* (FRO, 299grt/71) and *Ravnur* (FRO, 197grt/72). At the same berth, coasters such as the *Agenor* (DEU, 491grt/64) and *Passat* (DEU, 999grt/65) would deliver Volkswagen cars (typically VW Beetles in those days) from Emden. Frequent cargoes of acid from Belfast were also unloaded in the Edinburgh Dock. Vessels involved in this trade included *Onabi* (565grt/68) and *Odabo* (499grt/72), both registered in Bermuda, from Onabi Shipping Co and from Silver Chemical Tankers Ltd *Silvermerlin* (1259grt/68) and *Silverkestrel* (456grt/65). The Bilbao-registered *Fenol* and *Formol* (both ESP, 803grt/69) and *Metanol* (ESP, 803grt/70) were also used for acid imports.

An interesting vessel which docked close to the acid berth was the *Gardyloo* (1952grt/76), a purpose-built coaster employed by Lothian Regional Council to dispose of human waste. The name "Gardyloo" was used by servants in medieval Edinburgh to warn passers-by of waste about to be thrown from a window into the street below. The phrase was still in use as late the 1930s and 1940s, when many people had no indoor toilets. It is believed to have come from the French phrase "Gardez l'eau" (Mind the water) or possibly "Regardez l'eau" (Look out for the water). Ownership of the **Gardyloo** passed from the local authority to East Scotland Water in 1997 and Sea Gem International Ltd in 1999.

*The **Gardyloo** was photographed on 8 April 1978.*

Also in Edinburgh Dock, the **Richard Rahmann** (DEU, 424grt/64) was a regular caller with timber from Mantyluoto in Finland. The diminutive **Frigga Buur** and **Nanna Buur** (both DNK, 149grt/71) delivered stone chips from Elnesvaagen in Norway.

In the adjacent Albert Dock, a weekly general cargo service with Harlingen was operated. The writer recalls the **Westerdok** (NLD, 393grt/51) being used on this service in the early 1970s, later replaced by **Roelof Holwerda** (NLD, 383grt/61), a coaster which had a modern appearance for the era. Another visitor to the Albert Dock was **Ingi** (PAN, 650grt/55), bringing bottled beer from Germany, a commonplace commodity these days but quite exotic at the time.

On the opposite quayside, the container gantry crane installed in the late 1960s was used for the Macvan container shuttle service to Rotterdam, a history of which is provided by Colin Menzies in the June 2018 edition of *Coastal Shipping*. The first vessel the writer observed being loaded by the crane was the Sietas-built **Gala** (DEU, 499grt/68), which later became **Ala**, a coaster often mentioned in the pages of Coastal Shipping prior to being recycled. The **Nincop** (DEU, 499grt/68), also a Sietas Type 33 vessel, was a frequent visitor to Leith at the time. This smart coaster later became the **Alva** (VCT, 1037grt/68) which still visits Leith to this day loading red granite chips for Denmark, typically as back cargoes for her usual trading route bringing softwood from Varberg to Methil.

We mentioned earlier a general cargo service between Leith and Sullom Voe. This service was operated by the North of Scotland, Orkney & Shetland Shipping Company's **Rof Beaver** (1542grt/71). This coaster operated a weekly service from a roll-on/roll-off berth in the Albert Dock.

In Leith's Outer Harbour (also referred to in the past as the Albert Strait) a berth beside the Water of Leith swing bridge was used to import cargoes of china clay from Par. It was the coasters of J R Rix & Sons that typically brought the cargoes, including **Fylrix** (637grt/62), **Bobrix** (584grt/57), **Kenrix** (635grt/60) and **Jonrix** (647grt/57). The writer fondly recalls their distinctive green hulls and the white china clay dust covering the quayside. Coasters of the F T Everard fleet – such as **Centricity** and **Continuity** (both 655grt/55) - also delivered china clay but they usually unloaded in the Victoria Dock.

The Outer Harbour also contained a roll-on, roll-off ramp which was used for a weekly service between Leith and Gothenburg. Coasters from Elder Dempster Lines operated this service including the **Skyway** (1175grt/63), **Speedway** (1204grt/67) and **Clearway** (1160grt/70), the latter vessel having been built at Leith.

The construction of the Mills at Leith Docks took place as part of a wider development of the Western Harbour area. The Mills berth was very busy with coasters in the 1970s, with ships from the Tower Shipping, Mardorf Peach, Comben Longstaff and FT Everard fleets very much in evidence. Typical loading ports for the wheat cargoes included Hamburg, Rouen and Tilbury. Around this period the colliers of Stephenson Clarke also called at the Mills with wheat cargoes, including "flatirons" such as **Climping** and **Fletching** (both 1877grt/58). Imports of wheat to this berth continue today, though the suction elevators at the Mills have been replaced by grab discharge.

The largest dock at Leith is the Imperial Dock at the north of the port. During the review period of the early 1970s, regular imports of fertiliser were unloaded in the Imperial Dock, normally delivered by ships of the Metcalf Motor Coasters fleet, such as **David M** (452grt/57). Occasionally, cargoes of fertiliser were delivered by other veteran British coasters of the era, including **Frederick Hughes** (311grt/56), the Gloucester-registered **Fretherne** (351grt/50) and **Ferndene** (313grt/49), owned at the time by T G Irving of Sunderland and the subject of the "Coaster of the Past" feature in the August 2018 edition of *Coastal Shipping*.

Imports of pipes from Rotterdam were beginning during this period, regular callers being the **Roswitha** and **Joachim** (both DEU, 999grt/72) built at the Korneuburg shipyard far inland on the River Danube in Austria.

At the southern end of Imperial Dock, larger coasters would bring phosphate cargoes from Casablanca, the ships of the Christian Salvesen fleet often being involved, such as **Dunvegan Head** (4396grt/68) and **Duncansby Head** (4440grt/69). The same berth was used for imports of potash, often delivered by German coasters including

Burhaversand (DEU, 999grt/69), *Eckwardersand* (DEU, 1599grt/68) and *Beckumersand* (DEU, 1999grt/70), the latter vessel being converted to a livestock carrier in 1983.

Close to the entrance to the Imperial Dock was a tanker facility for the discharge of fuel and gas oil, typically delivered from Immingham, Fawley and Milford Haven. A regular and distinctive caller at this berth was the *Dangulf Maersk* (DNK, 3918grt/65). Ships of the Rowbotham fleet were also regular visitors with petroleum cargoes; they included *Anchorman* (795grt/62), *Pointsman* (2886grt/70), *Wheelsman* (2897grt/67), *Guidesman* (799grt/64), *Leadsman* (843grt/68), *Rudderman* (1592grt/68) and *Steersman* (1567grt/71). Another frequent visitor to the fuel depot was Stephenson Clarke's

Fernhurst (1525grt/61). The tanker berth closed some years ago.

Coastal shipping at Leith in the present day

The types of ship and cargoes handed have significantly changed over the years. The port itself has changed too, with areas such as the Victoria Dock and part of the Edinburgh Dock reclaimed for commercial developments. In the early 1970s, shipping enthusiasts had access to the entire port area and could view close-up the loading and unloading of the ships. Times have changed of course, but good photographic access can still be obtained at the Albert Dock, the Outer Harbour and, with a longish lens from the Ocean Terminal shopping centre, the Mills berth.

*Arriving with a cargo of grain from Norrkköping, The **Kaisa** (MLT, 3183gt/05) had just emerged from the entrance lock into the dock when photographed on 22 September 2012. An example of the Trader 4400 standard design from the Royal Bodewes shipyard at Hoogezand, she traded as **Aspoe** until 2008 and was renamed **Kaisa** following purchase by Hansa Shipping on 13 August 2008. The statue at the right of the image is one of several made by the artist Antony Gormley and placed at various points on the Water of Leith.*

(Laurie Rufus)

*An important export from Leith is malting barley which is taken to Islay for use in the famous distilleries on that island. Coasters from the fleet of Faversham Ships usually handle these cargoes and on 24 February 2017 we see **Victress** (BRB, 1512gt/92) with loading nearing completion.*

(Iain McGeachy)

An interesting vessel, the **Theoni S** (GRC,2405grt/58), ex **Marilor**-76, **Typhee**-69, was photographed in the north-east corner of Imperial Dock on 8 April 1978. She was discharging cargo from Dakar. She was built by Ateliers et Chantiers de Bretagne at Nantes and entered service as **Typhee** for French company Société Navale Caennaise. She was broken up at Hamburg in 1981.

(Bernard McCall)

Built by J W Cook & Co at Wivenhoe, Everard's **Celebrity** (582grt/76) is seen on the north side of Imperial Dock on 8 November 1980. She had arrived from Rotterdam two days previously and departed for the River Tees on the next day.

(Bernard McCall)

The Hugo Peters shipyard at Wewelsfleth built a series of stylish coasters for Günther Graebe, of Lübeck. She was one of several whose hull construction was subcontracted to Stader Schiffswerft because of the huge quantity of work at the Peters yard. The Stade yard had closed and was reopened for the construction of these hulls. She was launched as **Heidberg**, delivered as **Skeppsbron**, reverted to **Heidberg** in 1972 and became **Jenny Graebe** in 1978. She was berthed to the west of **Celebrity** with the Bredero Shaw pipe coating facility in the background.

(Bernard McCall)

Many of the trades observed in the 1970s have ceased. The liner/general cargo routes have gone, as has the container shuttle service to and from Rotterdam. Unsurprisingly, the waste disposal service provided by **Gardyloo** is no longer needed. Like any other ports, Leith has adapted to changing circumstances and continues to thrive, including many visits by oil support vessels and growing numbers of passenger ships outside the scope of Coastal Shipping.

In 2018, the usual import cargoes at Leith include significant volumes of agribulks. Regular shipments of wheat are unloaded at the Mills berth, coming from loading ports including Vierow, Wolgast, Hamburg, Tilbury and Harwich. Large quantities of maize are also imported – often by ships of the Arklow fleet – from French ports such as Blaye, Bordeaux and Tonnay Charente.

Other agribulk cargoes include cargoes of soya meal from Brake and gold corn gluten from Rotterdam – coasters often used for these imports include **H&S Wisdom** (NLD, 1552gt/04) and **Eems Delta** (NLD, 999gt/92).

In addition to wheat cargoes, the Mills berth in the Western Harbour is also used to unload deliveries of stone from Glensanda. The very large "coaster" **Yeoman Bank** (LBR, 24780gt/82) is often used to bring the stone cargoes, a vessel which ranks amongst the largest to visit the port. Recently, "proper" coasters such as **Aasli** (GIB, 3968gt/94), **Arklow Venture** (IRL, 2999gt/17), **Peak Bordeaux** (NLD, 2978gt/11) and **Fri Marlin** (BHS, 1990gt/94) have been used on this service.

Another cargo employing coastal shipping is cement, which is unloaded in the Imperial Dock. The usual loading port for these cargoes is Grimsby, coasters chartered for this service in recent years including **Union Gem** (IOM, 2230gt/91) and **Vedette** (IOM, 2545gt/00). At the time of writing, the cement imports have switched to larger vessels arriving from Alcanar in Spain.

Regarding exports, coated pipes continue to be shipped via purpose-built yellow gantry cranes in the Imperial Dock. Typically, coasters from Wilson Group and H&H Schiffahrts GmbH – such as **Transmar** (GIB, 2840gt/98) – have been employed in recent years to export the coated pipes. These cargoes are less frequent than in the past, though May/June 2018 saw several shipments loaded for St Petersburg by ships of the Rusich fleet.

Other common exports from Leith include red granite chips to Amsterdam and occasionally Danish ports, glass cullet to Figueira Da Foz , and barley to Port Ellen using the fleet of Faversham Ships. The Edinburgh Dock is seldom used for cargo-handling these days, an exception being occasional shipments of scrap loaded for ports in the south of England.

In conclusion, the port of Leith has a rich history of ship-building, ship-owning and cargo handling. It continues to be a port of great interest to ship enthusiasts.

Reference: *Port of Leith & Granton* by Graeme Somner, Tempus Publishing 2004

*Having discharged her cargo of cement, **Union Gem** begins to approach the lock at the start of a return voyage to Grimsby on 22 September 2012.* *She has awaited the arrival of **Kaisa** as seen on the previous page.*

(Laurie Rufus)

The **EMI Leader** (MLT, 2997gt/09) is berthed in the Outer Harbour on 23 September 2012, unloading maize from Bordeaux. Regular cargoes of maize continue to arrive at Leith but they are usually unloaded in the Imperial Dock. The pictured berth is now often used for export cargoes of red granite chips for Amsterdam. The image was taken from the Ocean Terminal shopping centre car park, a useful vantage point for ship photography at Leith.

(Alan Dowie)

The **Birch** (ATG, 1552gt/90) is pictured berthed in Leith's Albert Dock on 3 July 2010, unloading a cargo of pipes from Vlissingen. This coaster from the NYKI Shipping fleet was to return with further cargoes on 10 July and 21 August 2010. The pictured berth in the Albert Dock is where the container gantry crane was situated, serving the Macvan route to Rotterdam.

(Alan Dowie)

To the Heart of France

The River Rhône has been a vital communications route since Roman times but it was always a difficult and dangerous river. Improvements were made between 1885 and 1905 but the upstream sections of the river remained problematic. In 1933 the Compagnie Nationale du Rhône was established to develop the river for navigation, hydro power and irrigation. Twelve hydroelectric plants and associated locks were built between 1964 and 1980.

The river was originally a steep slope with rapids but the improvements have transformed it into a succession of gently sloping steps. It has thirteen reaches with an average length of 25km (15 miles) and the total length of the navigable Rhône is 330 km (205 miles). There are fourteen locks between the confluence of the River Rhône and River Saône at Lyon and the point where it flows into the Mediterranean at Port-Saint-Louis-du-Rhône.

The difference in level between Lyon and the sea is 62 metres (203 feet) and the rise / fall in the locks varies between 6.7 metres (22 feet) to 23 metres (75 feet). Although now largely controlled, there can be periods of strong flow rates and the speed of the current can exceed 3 metres per second in some areas. The CNR authorities keep a constant check on the flow rates along the whole length of the navigable river.

North of Lyon, the navigable waterway is the River Saône. From the town of Auxonne further north to the city of Lyon, the Saône waterway has been developed to allow the passage of vessels up to 3000 tonnes deadweight although in practice sea-going vessels do not sail north of Châlon-sur-Saône where there is a small basin used for cargo handling in addition to a couple of berths on the river .

*Our photographic journey along the Rhône and Saône will follow the route of the navigation from south to north. Ships wishing to make this voyage from the Mediterranean gain access to the Rhône via the port of Port-Saint-Louis-du-Rhône via a channel dug in 1871. In 1723 a tax was imposed on cargoes of salt and in 1737 the revenues raised were used for the construction of the Saint Louis Tower seen in the background of this view of **Coral Mer** (ATG, 1595gt/96) awaiting passage through to the Rhône on 1 October 2017.*

*The first major port to be noted on our journey north is Arles which comprises two quays, each able to accomodate two coasters simultaneously, on the eastern bank of the river. Both quays are rail-served and the port is justifiably proud of its role as a transhipment port. It currently handles almost half a million tonnes of cargo annually. On 31 July 2008. the **Bella** (VCT, 998gt/63) and **Natissa** (MLT, 1554gt/95) were noted at the southernmost quay. Also visible is a barge moored at a waiting berth. The presence of the latter vessel was very approriate as she was built by the Yorkshire Dry Dock Company as **Sea Rhone**.*

An important part of the improvements undertaken on the River Rhône was the construction of deviation canals where it would have been too difficult or even impossible to adapt the existing river for hydroelectric purposes. The longest of these is the Bollène deviation, 28 km (17 miles) in length. In the middle of this is Bollène lock, construction of which was completed in 1952. With its 23 metre rise/fall, it is the deepest lock on the river but despite its size it can be filled in only seven minutes. The huge size of the lock is evident as **Diamant** approaches on 2 September 2010. We shall see this ship again on the next page.

As we head north, our next significant port is Montélimar, once world renowned as the centre of nougat manufacture. This is no longer the town's key industry as the construction of the A7 autoroute (motorway) has meant that many tourists bypass the town on the way to and from the Mediterranean resorts and many factories have had to close. The single commercial quay is on the east side of a deviation and can handle two coasters simultaneously. The **Ace I** (VCT, 998gt/84) was photographed on 9 September 2007.

By far the most important port on the river is Lyon. The extensive dock area includes three covered terminals such as that seen here on 6 July 2010 with the **Mari Mer** (MLT, 1595gt/96) alongside. The port handles a wide variety of cargoes including containers, sand and aggregates, steel, agribulks, chemicals and petroleum products.

After the confluence of the River Saône and River Rhône south of Lyon, ships continuing their voyage north on the Saône pass through the centre of the city and past rows of properties of all kinds along the river banks. The **Tramontane** (BHS, 1423gt/83) passes cautiously upriver on 4 July 2010. Her outline may be familiar to some readers as she was built at Selby as **Stridence** for the London & Rochester Trading Company.

In this short survey we have concentrated on the industrial areas along the rivers. On 21 October 2017, the **Aquarius** (LTU, 1141gt/96) makes unhurried progress along the Saône above the city of Mâcon which gave its name to the nearby vineyards and "appelation".

With two crew members on the foredeck ready to put lines ashore, the **Diamant** (LTU, 998ft/85) approaches Châlon-sur-Saône on 24 September 2017, almost certainly to load grain which is a frequent export cargo for her.

(All photographs by Annemarie van Oers)

72